Cloud Computing
Facing the Reality

Ashwini Rath

BATOI PRESS

press.batoi.com

421, Saheed Nagar, Bhubaneswar 751 007 (INDIA)
Email: press@batoi.com

DEDICATION

To my grandfather

CONTENTS

ACKNOWLEDGMENTS

I acknowledge the atmosphere of optimism created by my near and dear ones making any effort in my life really smooth and easy. I appreciate the assistance and support by many people, knowingly or unknowingly, for making this book possible. I greatly value the discussion with my friends and colleagues who interacted with me for different IT projects during the writing of this book.

This book has seen working late in the evening and spending time away from my family; and I acknowledge their sacrifice, particularly my wife, Mita. It is also essential to note the contribution of my eight years-old son, Ayash, whose queries in his inimitable style while being told about 'cloud computing' have helped me stretch my imagination further and think of better examples. Above all, blessings and inspiration from my parents have made me work harder and better, an influence beyond any evaluation.

Ashwini Rath

PREFACE

If you do not hear or read that a company has adopted the "go cloud" strategy in their business plan, you feel the company is going in a wrong way! Weird thoughts? Yes, it is, but then it is a reality. It is also a fact that we, all, are using some or other IT resources on cloud on daily basis. In fact, there has been significant coverage about cloud computing in various research journals, and IT magazines, where people delve into various details of this novel computing paradigm, and try to educate us. All is well!

But what is this all about, and how can it effect a change in the landscape of computing in the coming days? What will happen with the organizations who have already invested their fortune in legacy systems? Will these new developments in computing alter the digital ecosystem, or will these synergize? Above all, what about the actual benefits of cloud computing and its contribution to our socio-economic evolution? In this rather small book, we shall discuss each of these aspects, and shall explore the new world of opportunities that come in our way with cloud computing.

I wish this book be a handy guide for IT users, solution providers, and public in general as I do not believe knowledge is a privilege to the few. I have taken care to make the conceptual aspects as simple as possible, and have tried to treat technical matters in a clear and lucid style.

Without much ado, let us get into business.

Yours Sincerely,

(Ashwini Kumar Rath)

1 INTRODUCTION

There are a number of seemingly-intriguing clichés associated with cloud computing. A marketing person cleverly claims that their product is cloud-based whereas the prospect unwittingly listens to hide his ignorance. You might have come across such situations, or will soon see such funny and unreasonable ones unfolding in front of your eyes. This is pure hype, the unusual expectations that ride over this new paradigm of computing. On the other hand, cloud computing is receiving wider acceptance, and new usable products are making their way with each passing day. These happenings have brought the issues associated with the current state of cloud computing, and the advantages it offers to the fore.

In this book, we shall review various aspects of cloud computing and its usages, and shall understand the challenges and opportunities it offers. After a general introduction about this computing paradigm in the first chapter, we shall discuss the actual definition in Chapter 2. We shall then go on to discuss the famous **Hype Cycle** vis-à-vis the realistic proposition that cloud computing offers in Chapter 3. Remaining portion of the book will cover the technologies involved (Chapter 4), the business models around cloud computing (Chapter 5), and finally its role in reshaping our individual, and collective, behaviors in recent times (Chapter 6). We shall end with a discussion about the opportunities and challenges that cloud computing offers (Chapter 7).

Moving forward with our plan to review the current status as the part of our general introduction, let us first discuss the pervasive nature of this term worldwide.

Cloud Everywhere

One day, I wanted to know how cloud computing has affected people using Internet. It may not be the best way; but certainly, an obvious way would be to test the search counts on Google. I was amazed by the result (figure 1.1).

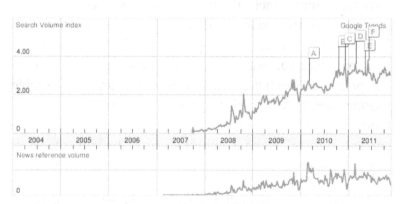

[Figure: 1.1: A Screenshot Carrying the Data on Google Trends]

The Google search with the phrase "cloud computing' returned about 129,000,000 results. The traffic surge is almost three times more than the average traffic scale (the scale based on the average worldwide traffic for the search term in all years), and this can be taken as an indicator of the popularity of cloud computing among general population.

I am not advocating the overwhelming acceptance of this computing paradigm by IT users just from the fact that there is an upswing in Google searches. Well, there are many things, which are popular on search engines; and it is difficult to ascertain the rationale behind. This index is an example rather of something that has attracted the attention worldwide; and encourages us to look into this further.

Trends We Live with

We have already given a couple of examples that exemplify the degree of hype surrounding cloud computing. And now, we shall provide a few practical examples that will illustrate the indispensability of cloud computing in present times. These will also provide an indicator of the acceptance of this computing paradigm across different categories of IT users.

Communication services like Gmail, Skype, WebEx, etc. (without bias towards any company, of course) have become so popular that many of us use these cloud services without knowing the details of their actual provisioning and management, and above all, about the much larger infrastructure behind these services.

Websites like Netflix, Bigflix, and Amazon Prime provide subscription-based access to thousands of videos by streaming these directly from their respective cloud infrastructures. Services like YouTube and Vimeo have revolutionized the way video sharing and promotion can happen. For example, regional scores like 'Kolaveri Di' could become an overnight hit across the globe just due to such robust cloud services that powered the online social media. The rapid accumulation of crowd-sourced content, a process that is considered as the part of Web 2.0 wave, has resulted in establishing major social media like Facebook, Twitter, etc.

It is not just about our personal and social activities. We use Google Apps, Microsoft Office 365, and Salesforce.com CRM (Customer Relationship Management) among others to carry out our general business activities. These applications have enabled us to access and manage our data while we are on move, and have almost eliminated the upfront cost of IT in our business.

I would like to point to another emerging area where the use of cloud computing has become inevitable. This is about controlling and managing devices and sensors remotely. This, of course, has an utility across different user categories. Individual consumers prefer to have an eye over their homes, and to control their home appliances when they are away – the homes are fitted with cameras that are linked to a cloud for streaming the videos on demand to the owner of household, and also to provide conditional alerts based on continual processing of images received from those cameras. Such computing scenarios are also applied in many areas like road traffic control, public security management, astronomical data processing, and environmental studies, etc.

An interesting example where the practical benefits have been reaped through the adoption of cloud computing is the Sharp Community Medical Organization, a non-profit group of 5000 independent physicians in San Diego County, California. They have leveraged a healthcare collaboration cloud where patients coordinate their care across physicians. The organization is now positioning to reward physicians when patients stay healthy. This example emphasizes the use of cloud services in social sectors. In fact, governments across the world adopt cloud services to avail benefits to their citizens faster, and to reduce the latency in bringing development to the respective regions (Chapter 6). Another feather in cap, adequate to generate further interests in studying about this new paradigm!

Of course, there are happenings that can also be disappointing. A big chunk of early adopters carrying unfulfilled expectations are getting upset. On the other hand, product developers and service providers have made it a point to associate cloud computing to virtually anything they offer, and refer to the name of cloud computing if their application or content is located at a central location and is accessed elsewhere. This makes our life more complex.

What's in a Name?

There is quite a bit of effort to trace the first use of the term 'cloud computing'. Though the reference of the name 'cloud' or even 'cloud computing' was not intended for exactly the same thing that we talk about these days, they can be used synonymously.

The first use of 'cloud' can be traced to an academic article at MIT, "The Self-governing Internet: Coordination by Design" (http://ccs.mit.edu/papers/CCSWP197/CCSWP197. html), where it referred to a large distributed cluster of computer networks. Later a company, NetCentric

Corporation that used to provide "carrier-class Internet fax technology," applied for trademark under application serial number 75291765 in 1998; but later abandoned it.

The word cloud was also used in an article, "An Internet Critic Who Is Not Shy About Ruffling the Big Names in High Technology" (http://www.nytimes.com/2001/04/09/techn ology/09HAIL.html?ex=1230872400&en=5d156fc75d40933 5&ei=5070), published in the New York Times, on April 09, 2001, to refer to the large network of computers. In this article, the author proposed that the Internet may be treated as a 'cloud' of computers.

However, the term cloud computing closest to what we refer to today, came to public when Eric Schmidt of Google used it to describe the software and server architecture as a service as envisaged by his company while talking to Danny Sullivan in the Search Engine Strategies Conference on August 09, 2006. Later Amazon used the term along with its product offerings, EC2 web services. What followed then became the notion that made it an inseparable form of computing, be in business, scientific or even for personal usages.

A Historical Perspective

As per the discussion in the last section about the initial usages of the term 'cloud computing', it only amounts to less than two decades. However, the sense of such computing model was founded long back - in the sixties when J.C.R. Licklider, one of the proponent of ARPANET (Advanced Research Projects Agency Network), introduced the idea of an "intergalactic computer network". In fact, the vision was to create an interconnected network to access program and data at any site from anywhere else on the globe, which was much like our current understanding about cloud computing.

Similarly, an American computer scientist, John McCarthy, is widely credited for proposing in sixties about the delivery of computation as an utility like a service bureau, a company which provides business services for a fee.

In fact, the evolution of cloud computing had begun since then. The grid computing had led the effort during the early period. Later, entrepreneurs began to exploit similar computing models in business scenarios as people started using internet bandwidth in their day-to-day life. On the other hand, it is worth mentioning a significant effort by the IT industry during the last decade of the 20th century, if we don't mention about the **ASP (Application Service Provider)** model where service providers kept the software rights with themselves, and rented out the software applications at the client-side. But then we were way behind the model that we called cloud computing.

The early adopter was Salesforce.com, which started delivering the CRM application in **Software as a Service (SaaS)** model, a model where a software application is delivered and managed centrally by the service provider, and is only available for use by consumers, who own their data and not the software. In the year 2006, when Amazon and Google started delivering their software and architecture as services, IT services got associated with large-scale delivery of computation, in terms of both program and data. All these comprise the basic tenet behind the evolution of the new paradigm of computing that consequently culminated into what we called 'cloud computing'.

Drawing Analogies

It is quite tricky to draw similarity between a bull and a horse even though they have something in common - they are mammals! Well, if that would serve the purpose of gaining insight into our object of study, it should be fine.

Let us consider a much cited example of travelling on an airplane. We could argue that one would prefer to purchase an aircraft, hire a pilot and crew, and also build the entire airport infrastructure to plan his or her flight schedule. Though a miniature percentage of population can still adopt this path, the general opinion will ridicule the proposition. People would rather avail similar, yet just adequate facilities, by buying a ticket with a fee from an airline. The airline company adopts a service model where the company is responsible to manage expensive assets, and to recruit and manage crew while offering services to passengers at a fee that is far below the capital investment and operation costs. Here, a passenger can avail service at a much lower cost compared to the earlier model of having a dedicated aircraft. At the same time, the airline company does profitable business by offering services to the large number of passengers. A win-win situation for both sides.

We can also discuss another popular example to bring in various important points to establish analogies with cloud computing better. This is about electricity that we consume daily at our homes, offices, and manufacturing plants.

The process of power generation, and building and maintaining its distribution network are big-scale activities in terms of both engineering and management. However, back home, we are neither concerned nor make ourselves aware of the entire supply-chain and the complexities involved in the process. We are not worried about the broader scale of operation or the costs involved. We are rather happy to use as it suites our requirements and budget; and we pay as per metered-usage.

People compare cloud computing to such service models. Well, yes it is correct up to this. Cloud computing proposes a large-scale computing system (hardware, network and software) that an IT vendor would establish and manage while providing all of these as services with a fee. But then, going further, it is a different service model, and it has its own unique characteristics and delivery mechanisms.

Need to Understand Better

The review of the current trends of cloud computing along with historical perspectives, has provided us a sense of significance about this new computing paradigm.

While it is easy to be carried away by hypes, a proper understanding will enable us to adopt the solutions in rightful manner and to maximize its benefits. This is our task in the next chapter.

2 UNDERSTANDING CLOUD COMPUTING

We talk of computation as a service bundle when we talk of cloud computing. We aim to use the entire platform, including server infrastructure, computer network, operating system and software applications, as a service; and aim to pay per-use basis. We pay a fee for the service, thus pay for use only.

As we discussed in the first chapter, the whole concept of 'Cloud Computing' started with using Software as a Service (SaaS) where application service providers setup their software applications to be used on pay-per-use basis from their central infrastructures. Later, the same concept was extended to infrastructure itself, and we called it as **IaaS** (Infrastructure as a Service). Similarly, we coined the term Platform as a Service (**PaaS**) that referred to the availability of a software platform as a service.

This inclusive approach to computing with hardware, software, and network, resources sourced from one or more vendors, located at one or more locations, and working in unison to provide highly available storage and applications, has led to the model of cloud computing. People also term this model as a technology though it can certainly be ascribed as a functional model with a bundle of intertwined (cloud) technologies. Thus the use of the term as a technology in this book or elsewhere must be understood in the right spirit.

A Search for Definition

As different providers provisioned their resources (software or hardware or both) and used the term cloud computing, people began to worry about the definition of this phrase. Different specialists and group of vendors started defining the term in different ways – as it suited their requirements.

At the same time, we cannot simply deny the contribution of these interest groups as the current understanding has made its way from those many trials, both wrong and right. Gradually dust settled with a standard definition being proposed by National Institute of Standards and Technology (NIST); and it received wide acceptance from providers, researchers and users alike. Let us now discuss this in detail.

A Model - the NIST Way

NIST proposed the model that can serve as a standard to understand various cloud services offered by multitude of cloud providers. The model is intended to serve as a means for broad comparisons of different cloud services and deployment methods. This also provides the basis to understand the whole paradigm, and to make the best use in business and common usages.

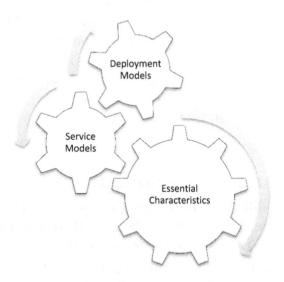

[Figure 2.1: Constituents of the Model of Cloud Computing]

As per the definition by NIST (http://csrc.nist.gov /publications/nistpubs/800-145/SP800-145.pdf), 'Cloud Computing' is a model for enabling convenient, on-demand network access to a shared pool of configurable computing resources (e.g., networks, servers, storage, applications, and services) that can be rapidly provisioned and released with minimal management effort or service provider interaction. The Cloud Model is composed of five **essential characteristics** (on-demand self-service, broad network access, resource pooling, rapid elasticity, and measured service), **three service models** (cloud software as a service or SaaS, cloud platform as a service or PaaS, and cloud infrastructure as a service or IaaS), and **four deployment**

models (private cloud, community cloud, public cloud, and hybrid cloud).

In the remaining part of this chapter, we shall discuss each item mentioned in this model and its impact in modifying the IT architecture.

Essential Characteristics

As mentioned above, cloud computing has five essential characteristics. We shall discuss these first, and shall then try to understand its influence on existing IT systems and their architecture:

1. **On-demand Self-service:** Before the advent of cloud computing, a major hurdle was to depend on a group of highly-skilled system administrators while provisioning and scaling IT resources, be it software, hardware or network. This was a slow and tedious process, and the turnaround time was sometimes pinching.

   With cloud computing, this capability has now fallen into the hands of users themselves sans the technical steps involved during the process. The proposition has also created a demand from providers to make each resource measurable, and to avail a simple user interface for the users to provision these resources when they require, on demand. The actual provisioning is supposed to be done at the level of software on service provider's side without human intervention.

2. **Broad Network Access:** Accessing cloud resource requires internet connectivity, and the definition

makes it explicit. The emphasis on broad connectivity and access promotes thin clients and platforms for accessing and using IT resources across different devices like desktop PCs, laptops, mobile phones and tablets. It addresses the need for universal access to IT resources as a part of cloud computing, a topic that we shall discuss in detail in Chapter 3.

3. **Resource Pooling:** The cloud computing promises an economic advantage through an optimal use of the available IT resources; and it is achieved by sharing resources between different tenants on demand. We set the stage for adopting a multi-tenancy model. Of course, the sharing process and intricacies are masked from the end-user, a step in concurrence with the above discussion about on-demand self-service.

4. **Rapid Elasticity:** This characteristic is consequential as we have automatic provisioning and scaling of IT resources possible on cloud. But, of course, it is now explicit and a major feature of cloud computing. It also implies to the availability of almost unlimited resources for allocation on demand. Though the term 'unlimited' can be misleading, availability of much more resources than usual collective demands from users makes a sense.

5. **Measured Service:** We have already talked about the need for measuring the resources, and thus services offered, while we discussed on-demand self-service above. It requires the cloud systems to employ a metering capability at some level of abstraction. The infrastructure services may use parameters like size of storage, unit of processing power, and incoming and

outgoing bandwidths for measuring the services offered. For example, Cloud Sites of Rackspace use compute cycle (abstract unit to measure computing resources) along with other obvious parameters like storage and bandwidth. Similarly, platform and software services may use parameters at an appropriate level of abstraction to create a usable measurement of services offered, like number of transactions, etc. Moreover, the metering facility at cloud systems requires creating dashboards and reporting facility for consumers who can monitor and adjust the allocation based on their requirements and budget.

After the above discussion, we can sense our changing view on using IT resources. A general user with a login access to cloud can allocate almost instantly as much resources as needed. Moreover, user can start using these resources from anywhere, anytime and with any device with a network connection. At the same time, the service provider manages the cloud system, which is equipped with tools for automated provisioning of resources, resource pooling for optimal shared usages, and for measurements and monitoring purposes. These measurement tools should be based on limited number of parameters for controlling allocation and usage of resources, and for receiving payment from users. A win-win situation for both sides.

We may now summarize our above understanding in the form of an illustration (figure 2.2) that describes the change to IT architecture in relation to the delivery and use of cloud services. The illustration shows augmentation of three new components to the IT system in the cloud computing environment. Let us review these one by one starting with the metering and billing tools.

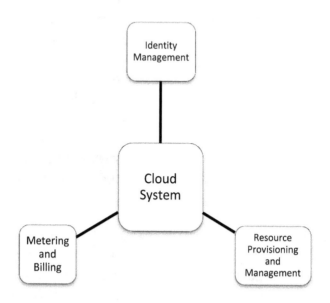

[Figure 2.2: Identifying New Components of a Cloud System Based on Its Five Essential Characteristics]

The metering and billing tools have two interaction points. One is tenant-facing where users can measure and monitor their resource usages, and can make payment for the purpose. The other interaction point of these tools is vendor-facing where the service provider can monitor, and manage the resource allocation and usage by tenants apart from tracking and managing the billing. Of course, such control is centrally managed on the side of service provider, and mostly without human intervention.

The second set of tools is meant to handle identities of users on cloud. It is the most important one from security point of view. These tools filter unwanted traffic at cloud, validate identity of rightful users, and assign appropriate access rights over the requested IT resources.

The final set of tools is meant for provisioning of resources on demand and their management. These are basically back-end management tools automating crucial tasks at service provider's end. These do not require human intervention except during certain typical system administration activities or in special circumstances. In fact, a major role of these tools comes into picture when there is a failure within the system. And, then the automatic recovery of the system should be the handiwork of these tools. We shall discuss more about the causes and types of system failures, and also relevant aspects related to their automatic recovery in Chapter 4.

Alternatively, we can understand that a cloud system must have these three sets of tools built into its architecture; and that is what the five cloud characteristics propose apart from some best practices for delivering and using cloud resources. Some of the implied best practices for cloud service providers that are worth mentioning here:

- Availability of simple and usable user interface for users to provision and manage IT resources they require

- Automation is the key – the system should be able to run and serve its users without no or least human intervention at service provider's end

- The IT resources must always be available on network and for universal access by its rightful users

- Cloud system must be able to allocate additional resources for resource intensive requirements by any user any time while making optimal utilization of all available resources.

- The IT resources must be quantified in an unambiguous manner, and must be measurable with a limited number of parameters.

It is important to incorporate all the best practices into the design, deployment and delivery of cloud services.

Now, continuing our discussion, we must note that the cloud characteristics bring some radical changes to the way both physical and software architectures are conceived within a cloud system. Cloud service providers adopt appropriate ways to sync with these requirements at all levels, and adhere to the best practices laid while designing, deploying and delivering their cloud services. In the next section, we shall discuss these levels of service delivery as different service models of cloud computing; and shall postpone the discussion about deployment models to a section after that.

Service Models

The definition proposes three service models. Let us review these three in detail first, and then discuss their impact on IT architecture:

1. **Software as a Service (SaaS):** We have already discussed this in different places while scanning through the history of computing in the Chapter 1 and also at the start of the current chapter for introducing the concept of cloud computing.

Basically, service providers offer their software applications as services in this model of IT delivery. Service providers manage all aspects of software including data backup and restore apart from its maintenance and upgrades. Moreover, they manage underlying hardware and network resources for end-users to use software applications oblivious of the backend management. Salesforce.com has been an early player in this tier of services as we have discussed in Chapter 1. Similarly, Wordpress.com can be considered as another example where usages go beyond business domain. There have been numerous other software service providers specialized in different verticals who are gradually shifting or cloning their software applications as cloud services, thus becoming SaaS providers.

2. **Platform as a Service (PaaS):** These are basically the kind of services useful for developers and solution providers. Such services provision development environments, and avail programming libraries, thus expediting the process of application development. These also provide tools for quick deployment and maintenance of software applications. A platform must be capable of handling administrative tasks like updating OS patches, upgrading supporting software hosted on it, and managing and scaling network resources automatically. Major players for this tier of services are Microsoft (with its Azure Cloud Computing platform) and Google (with Google App Engine). On the other hand, many new PaaS offerings are coming to the market using different open source

technologies and innovative development frameworks based on those.

3. **Infrastructure as a Service (IaaS):** This remains at the core of a cloud system where service provider avail servers, storage devices and network resources for use as services. Cloud infrastructure equipped with different software tools like **hypervisor**, and **cloud orchestration toolkits** (both to be discussed in Chapter 4), provides an interface between the users and the actual physical infrastructure. These tools help manage and deliver infrastructure as a service. Rackspace and Amazon are two prominent players in this tier of cloud services though almost all primary web hosting companies have made their foray into this service model in the recent years.

[Figure 2.3: A Few Major Products in Three Service Models]

On the other hand, it is important to note that the same provider can very well encompass all the three tiers. Also, different companies offering services in different tiers (service models) can create a larger ecosystem. For example, Microsoft provides its Azure in PaaS model whereas its Windows Azure and SQL Azure in SaaS model. Similarly, Rackspace provides its cloud services in IaaS model, and many other providers, who deliver in PaaS or SaaS model, have built their offerings based on Rackspace's infrastructure, and, thus creating a large ecosystem of cloud.

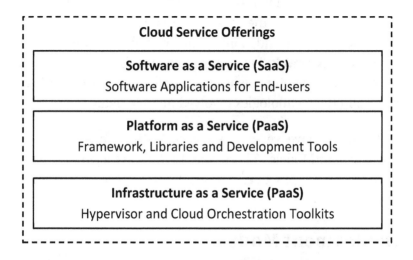

[Figure: 2.4: Illustration of Three Service Models]

I would not like to go into the details of history when many different service models were being proposed, like **HaaS (Hardware as a Service)** and **NaaS (Network as a Service)**, etc., as they eventually fall under above three broad categories. Rather, we should take solace from the consolidation of thoughts and emergence of a set of comprehensive, yet distinct, cloud service models, which can be used then for building a highly modular architecture of IT systems ready to be delivered as a service. These service models bring in changes to IT systems where different tiers of services can be conceived; and provide excellent means to classify and describe relevant technologies.

The above illustration (figure 2.4) shows the augmentation of a software stack into the cloud system exactly the way we had discovered how three sets of software tools were accommodated into a cloud system while discussing on the essential characteristics of cloud computing and their impact on architecture. We shall take this illustration as the basic means to classify different technologies on cloud, and would call this as the **Cloud Technology Stack**. Let us postpone any further discussion on this until Chapter 4 where we shall cover the technology stack and the technologies involved in great detail.

Well, we have yet another aspect still left; and that is 'Deployment Models'. These refer to the ways a cloud system is deployed in practice. Let us discuss these in the next section.

Deployment Models

There are four deployment models as proposed by the NIST definition. The deployment of a cloud system in different ways influences the way the cloud system is configured, and the IT services are delivered to users. This significantly alters the architecture of IT system as it is evident from our above discussion. Let us review each one before we discuss their impact on architecture:

1. **Public Cloud:** This is the de facto deployment model when people refer to a cloud service. Rackspace Cloud, Amazon AWS, and Microsoft Azure

are typical examples of large public cloud. The success of such deployment model relies heavily on its scalability and availability.

2. **Private Cloud:** We come across many organizations where circumstances and business terms decide about keeping the data on premise or somewhere else but in private. These two parameters have been addressed through a deployment model called private deployment of cloud or a private cloud. Here, IT resources are meant to be used by an organization exclusively. The management aspects may be kept within the organization or be outsourced to 3rd parties, but the guarantee for dedicated service must be honored. Also, the infrastructure may be maintained on premise, or may be located at 3rd party location(s) as long as the exclusive usage is guaranteed.

3. **Community Cloud:** Different communities, who have shared objectives and requirements, would also demand specific computing environments and applications. These are met through the deployment of cloud system where only the members of the community use it. This is obvious due to the availability of features that suit the community's specific needs. Google provides App Engine platform, which basically targets Python programmers; and Zend provides a cloud platform for PHP community. There is a distinct advantage for the community where members prefer specific tools and technologies to build their IT solutions on the top of respective platforms. Please note that the offerings on a community cloud can span all three service models in

general though we have given a few specific examples only.

4. **Hybrid Cloud:** This deployment model is a mixture of two or all three other cloud deployment models. In this case, certain components of the cloud system will be located in the public cloud, some other in private cloud, and perhaps, the remaining ones in community cloud as suited. The decision of choosing the deployment of different subsystems lies on business terms, and accessibility requirements among others (to be discussed in detail in Chapter 5). The major areas of emphasis while dealing with hybrid cloud is to handle the partitioning issues; and we shall discuss these in detail in Chapter 4.

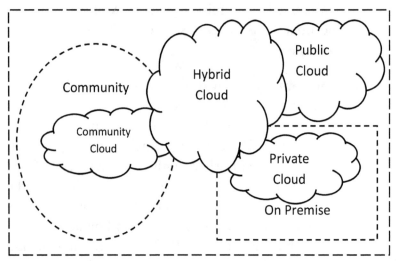

[Figure 2.5: Illustration of Four Deployment Models]

The illustration (figure 2.5) depicts different deployment models, and in particular, signifies the complexities that a hybrid cloud can bring in during building and managing such cloud system. It is to be noted that any of the deployment models does not put any restriction on locating the parts of a cloud system in different geographical areas. Rather, it becomes essential for cloud systems to exist in a distributed manner to enable redundancy and quick delivery of data to users (we shall discuss more on this in Chapter 4).

Now that we have learnt about the NIST definition in full, we are equipped with ingredients to relook at the IT service architecture. We shall discuss about our changed perspective in the following section.

A Renewed Perspective

We have shifted our attention from discrete systems that are managed by manual efforts of the highly skilled staff of a service provider to an automated self-managed service that can be provisioned and consumed on demand. We have also moved from the scenario of using enterprise systems on specialized terminals to one that promotes universal access by the user with appropriate access privileges.

Data are now stored in a distributed manner, so also the computing assets. This distribution can be organized into virtualized compartments (**Virtual Machines, or VMs**) in a bigger machine or across different machines located in a single location or spread across different geographical locations (to be discussed in detail in Chapter 4). Limit is not drawn here; the systems engaged in this distributed conglomeration can be disparate too if circumstances demand, i.e., these systems can operate and be managed differently, but adhere to the same set of standards and protocols while talking to one another. This is the concept of

distributed computing, and this is what cloud computing proposes too.

Cloud computing, as it is known, starts with a large-scale (how large, it depends on context) central computing infrastructure, sitting within one or more datacenters. Powerful server machines and other devices scale together with a principle called **virtualization** to provide a uniform hardware platform. Cloud applications or **Apps** function from this mega computing platform equipped with networking to communicate with the external world. These apps are supported by automated management tools, and are available for users to access and use from their client devices. Here the client device can be a desktop or a mobile device equipped with a thin client, like browser, and internet connectivity.

The above description has been illustrated in the figure 2.6 where access to Apps is controlled by the augmented tools that we have discussed earlier. Users register their identities on the central cloud system, and this identity is critical to access and consume IT resources by the users on cloud. The identity is verified while accessing the cloud services, and the user access is linked to the Metering and Billing tools while the allocation and usages of resources are actually controlled through Resource Provisioning and Management tools.

The universal access to resources and the sharing of computing resources, while retaining the privacy of data, demand a thorough review of the security architecture too. The security is enforced by the cloud system by allowing access to the appropriate **user roles**, and restricting the access from other roles that do not have the requisite privileges. This is usually implemented through one of the **RBAC (Role Based Access Control)** schemes, which we shall discuss further in Chapter 4.

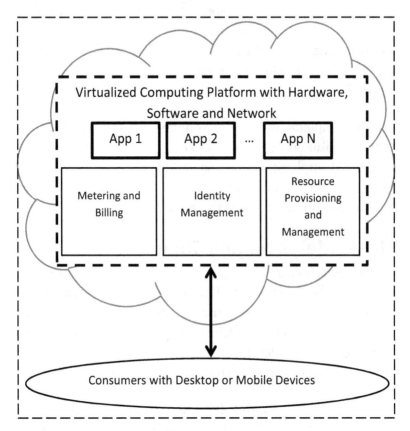

[Figure 2.6: The Cloud IT Service Architecture]

Similarly, at infrastructure level, unwanted traffic within the virtual hardware platform is restricted, and only traffic following appropriate rules are allowed. This consistent view across different levels provides a clear understanding of the cloud architecture, and gives an insight into the security implementation.

The above discussion and review of the underlying scenarios unfold various aspects in the entire cloud delivery cycle. The new perspective is inclusive, which means that the existing solution providers and programmers should be able to use their existing knowledge and expertise on standard programming tools. Basically, migration must be smooth and the effort should be minimal. We shall discuss more on this in Chapter 5.

While implementing cloud systems, different vendors use various situation-specific jargons apart from some specialized implementations as suited. We shall not discuss these in this book, and rather leave those to the documentation of the respective cloud systems.

The Model Is No Red Tape

The definition by NIST proposes a broad model of cloud usage and best practices. This promotes a functional IT service architecture that can meet diverse needs of users. Moreover, it provides guidelines for cloud service providers to create standardized facilities that can meet expectations from users, and to optimize overall costs on their side too.

On the other hand, this definition cannot undo the speed of innovations by red-taping the evolution in our thinking based on user demands and available possibilities to match these. We shall dedicate the next chapter for reviewing the ground realities in IT, expectations from users, and challenges in front of service providers to understand the state of cloud computing in practice.

3 TIME TO GO CLOUD: HYPE TO REALITY

A plum of happiness spreads over the face of an IT consultant when an inquisitive customer enquires about the cloud computing. A sense of faith is bestowed upon the consultant by customer to get the right solution, and perhaps, the today's solution. In the same breath, the consultant embarks upon the difficult task of providing IT solution with right platforms and Apps drawn from the mushrooming industry with a large number of cloud-based IT providers, some claiming 'go cloud' to anything they offer while others having complicated proprietary solutions. Both are bad for customer, and consequently dent the credibility of the consultant.

On the other hand, the hype of cloud computing has the capability to drive the decision-making at board meetings. A single-person enterprise finds it lucrative to settle with a few cloud providers to meet their different business needs to avoid upfront investment in IT. Even common people hook to the cloud for news, entertainment, education and research.

Yes, we have discussed the hype in the Chapter 1. In fact, the hype surrounding cloud computing has hindered its rightful adoption and exploitation. In this chapter, we shall review the famous Hype Cycle, and predictions and happenings related to the cloud computing paradigm. We shall draw parallels to a historic phenomenon of automobile industry, and shall then review the changes to IT landscape in the past several decades to understand the realistic shift towards adopting this novel computing paradigm.

The Famous Hype Cycle

Hype Cycle (figure 3.1) is a graph of the visibility of a technology in the course of time.

[Figure: 3.1: The Famous Hype Cycle for Technologies]

It is a general phenomenon that a technology, when appears in market, generates a greater hype or unusual attention than many times justified, taking the visibility of the technology to its peak, known as the **peak of inflated expectations**, from the initial appearance or point of **technology trigger**. However, as time proceeds, the technology gets feedback from users; and further innovations take place due to efforts by providers and makers of the technology to meet users' demands thereby bringing the technology to a practical stage of rightful adoption and appropriate usage. This is known as the **plateau of productivity**.

However, the interesting aspects of this transition of technology from high visibility to a realistic regime of successful adoption and productivity lie prior to the final realization. In the course of occurrence of such transition, the visibility dives down initially exerting pressure on providers and makers of the technology to innovate rapidly. This phase is known as the **trough of disillusionment** after the expectation from users falls as rapidly as it went up as innovations struggle to match. Then industry innovates; and it gradually pushes the acceptance of the technology among users slowly, taking the visibility through the **slope of enlightenment** and reaching the plateau of productivity finally.

Cloud Computing is going through such a hype cycle. As per "Gartner's Hype Cycle for emerging technologies published in 2011", cloud computing was nearing the trough of disillusionment (figure 3.1); and the next two to five years will see its consolidation among users bringing it into the mainstream adoption and full exploitation. In fact, cloud computing is set to traverse the similar path like any other technology due to the mismatch in innovations required at the backdrop of unusual expectations generated among users.

Here, we shall not argue about the exact timeline as formulated in the Gartner's predictions. We shall rather view the scenario holistically with competing factors of users' demands and innovations that will gradually guide the rightful adoption of this technology.

User Demands and Innovations

It is not a solitary situation for cloud computing, and not even for IT, where user demands drives innovations. In fact, the complex interplay of these two competing forces determines the fate of a technology. An optimistic scenario occurs when innovations by providers match the demands from users. On the other hand, adoptability suffers when reverse thing happens. While discussing the Hype Cycle in the previous section, which describes the entire lifecycle of a successful technology, we have seen the crest and trough of visibility of the technology, and later a productive phase of its adoption by target users.

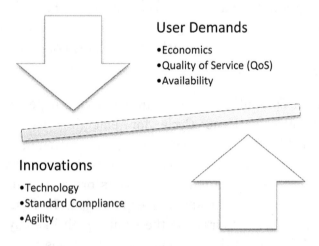

User Demands

• Economics
• Quality of Service (QoS)
• Availability

Innovations

• Technology
• Standard Compliance
• Agility

[Figure: 3.2: User Demands versus Innovations]

Now let us look into these two competitive forces, user demands and innovations, in detail (figure 3.2) that continually balance the industry scenario with respect to the adoption and use of a particular technology.

It is a complex process, after all, as the verdict is the result of a collective phenomenon. Consumers settle for economics always, in fact, for the best possible option. When the technology is nascent, the cost of a product using the technology is high, and thus a premium price tag is not surprising. However, widespread adoption can only happen with cost falling back into an affordable limit. And, the limit is determined by different economic indices.

Apart from economics, other factors like **Quality of Service (QoS)** and availability are critical in determining the fate of a product using the technology in question. QoS is a broad term encompassing several different aspects of a service including usability, and guarantee of service, etc. In layman's term, usability pertains to how easy it is to use a particular technology or a product using this technology, and its different features. Guarantee of service requires Service Level Agreement (SLA) over a mere advertised claim of service provider about meeting users' demands in applicable situations. On the other hand, availability of a product is realized if users can access and use the product whenever and wherever its demand arises.

The competitiveness of a technology or of a product using the technology is ascertained based on how well it serves the above parameters. To understand the adoptability of a product, it is essential to get feedback from users when they use the technology. And, feedback acts as the driver for the future innovations by the providers and makers. On the other hand, innovations rely on parameters like technology, standard compliance, and agility of the product to different possible usage scenarios.

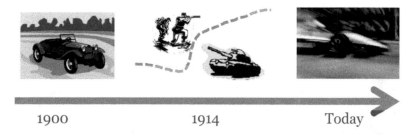

| 1900 | 1914 | Today |

[Figure 3.3: Automobile Industry: A Century-old Phenomenon]

To elaborate the above concepts and to consolidate our thoughts further, let us look beyond IT, and scan through the historic happenings in automobile industry since late 19th century which has seen an evolution spanned over a century (figure 3.3).

During the late 19th century, thousands of automobile design and manufacturing units were operating. However, the process of designing and manufacturing was mostly manual. The production cycle was long and costly. As the technology and methods were yet to mature, imparting skills to large workforce and upgrading their skills continually was a difficult and costly proposition too. Only a few automobiles could be produced from a manufacturing plant every year. Consequently, the costs of automobiles attracted high price tags; and were thus accessible to ruling establishments and economically privileged population.

As expectations from business opportunities went up, entrepreneurs started new ventures along the supply line starting from getting raw materials, actual production and building of manufacturing tools to delivering the automobiles to target users. Also, engineers, technicians, creative people and even common workers got attracted towards this industry for higher remunerations. This resulted in larger manpower pool, and created a sense of chaos in the absence of standard process of production across different companies. The situation led to disappointments when the expectations did not match with the ground realities.

Here, it is noteworthy to mention about a major event. This was when World War I started in Europe. The requirements of automobiles to supply weapons and support materials to soldiers at battlefront increased. More tanks and other vehicles were needed, and were expected to be available on demand, and, of course, to be very usable. Giving a mundane example, let us evaluate a scenario when bolt of a vehicle needed replacement in the enemy territory. It was a choice between contacting the original vendor, and adopting a solution where the accessories are standardized and available elsewhere irrespective of the vendor who manufactured those. Innovations in this front led to adopting a standardization process that was later provided impetus to ISO standards.

The need for large number of vehicles triggered the requirement for quicker production process. This resulted in innovations in automobile engineering, and in the process of production. Today, multiple vehicles come out of a modern plant every minute; and consequently, there is significant reduction in cost and enhancement in quality. Moreover, common usages and fast changing lifestyles of users brought the subtle parameter of agility into the design, manufacturing, delivery and re-engaging users' feedback into the next cycle of production process.

The above example vindicates our proposition about requirement for lower cost, standardization of product, improved quality and faster production process. It also illustrates the approach to technology development leading to fruitful acceptance by users.

Can we apply the same paradigm into our understanding of the changing scenarios in IT? The answer is 'yes'. To substantiate this, let us look again into history, though not as early as the previous example.

Phenomenon Repeats

Let us review the evolution of IT briefly, pattern of its adoption by users and the consequent influence on innovations. Well, we must note that feedback cycle is faster today; and the technology must keep pace to this shrinking cycle to mature, to be productive, and above all, to be adopted successfully among its target users.

Information Technology started presenting a complex landscape due to its impact not only on every sphere of business, but also due to the radical changes in human behavior and the multitude of dependencies on different other technologies. Though these complexities have challenged the entire human fraternity, the quicker adoption and ubiquitous usages have propelled the need for better economic proposition and high level of simplicity in its usage.

Before 1990, application of IT was largely limited to using LAN-based software system where a huge (in fact, it was huge in size) and all-powerful machine was running the software, and was meeting all computing needs of the enterprise. Consumers of IT used to take help of dumb terminals to access the software system on this large central machine. That was mainframe era.

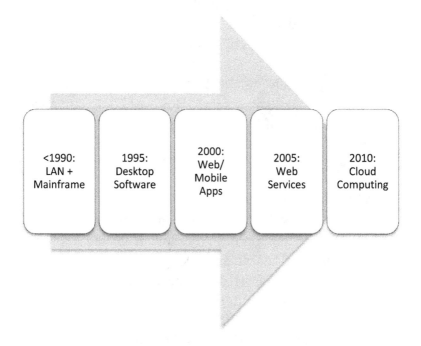

[Figure: 3.4: Timeline of Evolution in IT]

In 1990's, personal computers (PC) became popular; and those dumb terminals were replaced by these new powerful machines sitting near the users. Thus started the PC era, when numerous desktop software applications were written and used in a big way. Of course, LAN computing continued to be the carrier of enterprise-wide IT.

Towards the end of last century, widespread internet usage showed new ways to use software applications. Many web and mobile applications were developed. New scripting languages, database systems backed by open source movement played a significant role in keeping the momentum of innovations up in IT. Methods of collaboration and information management saw transformations with tactically planned deployment of geographically distributed IT resources that would reside partly within the LAN environment, and the remaining on web servers. In such situations, web applications mostly acted as extensions to the legacy applications, and were usually treated light-weight. However, the apparently separated islands of LAN ecosystem found channels of the Internet to work in tandem with one another. The barrier was broken.

With this new opportunity, many new possibilities emerged. This period saw faster innovations in different fronts. The entire cycle of IT fulfillment incited many new developments. Datacenters adopted energy efficient technologies, and invested in the automation of system administration and monitoring. Users could afford servers at lower cost. Open source scripting languages like PHP and database systems like MySQL gained immense popularity among application developers giving rise to a large community, and numerous innovative and popular applications. This enabled greater competition, thereby reducing the cost of application development.

IT became ubiquitous, and expectations went high regarding economics, QoS and availability. On the other hand, the critical issues and shortcomings became more prominent with increased adoptability of IT, and the availability of applications for almost every usage scenario. Business users (and enterprises) continued (or even increased) their dependence on developers to integrate various solutions, and to manage it on-premise. The cost of hiring developers subsequently increased; and it was unsustainable as an individual developer or freelancer may not be as reliable as an IT service company due to the possibility of the changes in their priorities or careers, or even location change apart from many other extreme possibilities. On the other hand, the option of hiring enterprises could only come at a premium price as service companies had to manage all these risks. It was no win-win situation though both end-users and the service providers accepted the situation and marched ahead. And, everybody waited for the next major innovation.

Onsite software and user-specific custom software development became untenable due to the higher cost of development and management. This phenomenon, in fact, triggered the adoption of SaaS model. Even though this provided limited scope for customization of applications, consumers were not bothered about initial (upfront) cost of software, its upgrade cost, or even high maintenance cost and risks. They could rather use software applications with minimal subscription fees while the service provider owned these. This was a win-win situation where provider did not have to maintain multiple copies of application at multiple locations (without direct control over the system as those were sitting on customer's premises), thus reducing the overall cost of management of application life-cycle.

Different software applications with their own architecture, and data storage and manipulation mechanism offered an uphill task for inter-communications. This triggered the need for a standard way for applications to talk to one another, i.e., to access data from one another. The result is the popular acceptance of standard protocols for **Application Programming Interface (API)**.

The above development was important as it encouraged thinking of software applications as a conglomerate of disparate systems communicating with each other through standard API – the concept of **Web Service** was born. Web service evolved as an encapsulation of data and access methods adhering to standard protocols like SOAP, XML-RPC and ReST, and exchanging data with one another through standard formats like XML and JSON. We shall learn more about these standards in Chapter 4 when we define and discuss software technologies in today's context.

Gradually, we entered into the era of cloud computing. It is not a single step development from the earlier stage; rather, it was multi-fold. However, things which remained constant through different periods are the mutually engaging parameters like user demands and innovations.

Now, we need to understand the inevitability and essence of cloud computing with respect to these fundamental parameters, user demands and innovations, in the following section.

Economics of Accessing Big Data

We shall confine our discussion to three prominent demands from users, and the innovations driven by these: **big data**, **universal access**, and **economies of scale** (figure 3.5). These can be called as the major drivers of cloud computing today. On the other hand, the paradigm of cloud computing can be called as the result of economics of accessing big data universally.

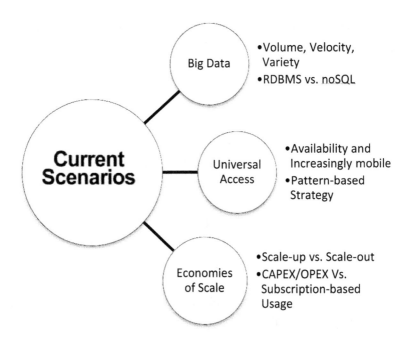

[Figure 3.5: Three Major Drivers of Cloud Computing]

With the increasing usage of web services, websites could be scalable easily with least redundancy of development and maintenance efforts, and without promoting a monolithic architecture. As Web 2.0 wave spread, content piled up at websites. This created a challenge to manage data of large scale. Data size of Terabyte then became usual; and went up to Petabyte, and Exabyte, scales easily. In the first chapter of this book, we have discussed about large video content, such as movies and surveillance camera outputs, being handled in day-to-day life by us – these are also about data of these scales. To give another example, Walmart handles more than a million customer transactions every hour; and this data, having an approximate size of 2.5 Petabytes, is equivalent of 167 times the total information contained in all the books in the US Library of Congress! The data of such a magnitude are known as big data.

The name 'big data' cannot be confused with just large size or volume of data; rather, it has other quantitative attributes like velocity (the speed of data storage and retrieval) and variety (the varieties of data that are created and used). The traditional Relational Database Management Systems (RDBMS) and associated tools, which were being used to manage data since long, fail to provide adequate means to handle big data. Thus an alternate data management system, known as **noSQL (not only SQL)**, came into the picture. We shall defer the formal definition of big data and a technical discussion on this topic until the next chapter.

On the other hand, we are increasingly going mobile in our personal and professional lives. In such situations, we expect to acquire the capability to access our data and any public information from anywhere, at any time and with any device having a network connectivity. This expectation of having a universal access to big data signifies the changing mindset, and drives innovations. We shall discuss on technologies related to user devices and cloud clients in Chapter 4.

Moreover, the availability of big data and accessing these universally have their influences on analytics, the faculty of developing optimal recommendations based on insights into data. Analytics use statistical models, and analysis against existing or simulated future data or both to arrive at decision making. This approach is popularly known as **pattern-**

based strategy. Each cycle of analytics is based on seeking a pattern from the available data, modeling the impact, and finally, adapting according to the patterns.

A few years back, this was a separate process of drawing data from slower tape drives, and processing these through complex programs at periodic intervals to seek patterns or trends. It was like answering questions like what happened and why it happened – an era of **Old Analytics**.

However, we now expect data to be available anytime, in real time. We cannot afford to store our data in slower devices, and thus, to reconcile with our traditional queries while dealing with analytics. We are more interested to know what is happening now, and what can happen next – a shift from the thinking of Old Analytics. These renewed expectations have paved the way for pattern-based strategy to go real-time, in business or elsewhere.

Real-time analytics demands the access and processing of big data for any meaningful purpose, and requires large-scale computation and highly available storage that must be economic too. The option of deploying a single big server with larger computing power or a single disk with larger storage to match this scale (known as vertical scaling or scaling up) becomes untenable as systems would quickly reach their limits of technical-feasibility. The alternative approach is to have a distributed environment where usual low-end servers and storage devices are linked horizontally (horizontal scaling, or scale-out) to create a mammoth computing system. Well, we are talking about cloud computing!

Today, people emphasize on reducing the time gap between a plan and its materialization or Time to Value (TTV), and the Total Cost of Ownership (TCO) while making a decision on IT investment. Thus, the subscription-based usage model has become popular as it facilitates instant use of IT resources, eliminates the capital expenditures (CapEx), and curtails operational expenditures (OpEx).

We have seen the inevitability of cloud computing in the changed scenario involving big data. Basically, this can be understood as achieving the economy of scale for providing universal access to big data that we incessantly generate these days.

Growth in Cloud Adoption

With a strong advocacy for cloud computing based on ground realities of today, it would be justified to know about the adoption of this computing paradigm in practice.

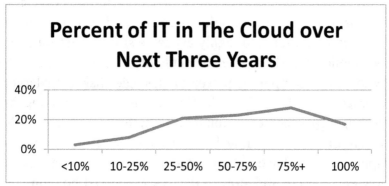

Figure 3.6: Symbolic Representation of Cloud Computing Adoption Rate.
(Ref: Article by Balakrishna Narasimhan and Ryan Nichols in March 2011 Issue of Computer, IEEE Computer Society. The Horizontal Axis Denotes the Percentage of Respondents)

The above illustration has been used to denote the trend in a symbolic way. In fact, there are many surveys with distinct trends that establish faster adoption, even substantial increase in the rate of adoption, and above all, a very positive scenario. Let us now scan through some important data from different surveys that provide insights into the adoption of cloud computing in various spheres:

- As a report of Redshift Research (http://www.amd.com/us/Documents/Cloud-Adoption-Approaches-and-Attitudes-Research-Report.pdf) suggests, 54% of business and 27% of government prefer private cloud solution. Public cloud adoption would be 9% and 17% respectively; similarly, hybrid cloud adoption would be 5% and 7% respectively.

- CDW 2011 Cloud Computing Tracking Poll (http://www.cdw.com/shop/tools/surveys/survey.asp?SurveyKey=D808B2971F634B5A96E452FE7E6FA165) brings out figures for IT adoption in the USA as 21% for SMEs, 37% for large businesses, 29% for federal government, 23% for state and local governments, 30% for healthcare, 27% for schools and 34% for higher education.

- Asia-Pacific Business and Technology Report (http://www.biztechreport.com/story/1202-cloud-services-asia-pacific-region) informs that the cloud computing market in Japan will grow to U.S.$29.2 billion by 2015.

- SMB Cloud Adoption Study Dec 2010 by Microsoft points that 39% of SMEs would be paying for one or more cloud services within three years.

We shall discuss more on the migration to cloud, and adoption scenarios in Chapter 5. Let us now proceed to summarize the success path of cloud computing and plan our next discussion topics.

Following the Path of Success

Through the current chapter, we explored the hype and realities around the paradigm of cloud computing from the perspective of collective interplay between demands from the vast group of IT users and innovations across the mushrooming industry supporting the growth. We discussed the present scenario from the point of view of big data, universal access requirements and economies of scale.

While it is a happy situation all along with optimistic examples and analyses, it is imperative to learn the key technologies that are responsible for this renewed perspective. We shall discuss these in the next chapter before we again return to applications of this new paradigm for remaining part of the book.

4 THE TECHNOLOGY LANDSCAPE

We have had adequate talk about the realistic foundation of cloud computing as a new way of delivering IT services. This talk will remain tangential if we do not understand the technologies that play cardinal roles in shaping this novel computing paradigm. In this chapter, we shall discuss the key underlying technologies. We shall refer to some of the major vendor-specific technologies and products (when appropriate) as examples without creating bias, and shall retain the thread of discussion about the fundamental aspects of this computing paradigm.

To come down to actual discussion, we shall maintain our reference to the same NIST definition discussed in Chapter 2. We shall utilize our acquired knowledge about the way cloud computing being characterized, being treated as different services, and the ways of deployment. As a matter of convenience, we shall view cloud computing from the perspective of three categories of services (service models), and shall stack all requisite technologies and other components around these (Cloud Technology Stack as we had mentioned in Chapter 2). Figure 4.1 illustrates this technology stack – an organized view of the technologies used to build a cloud ecosystem.

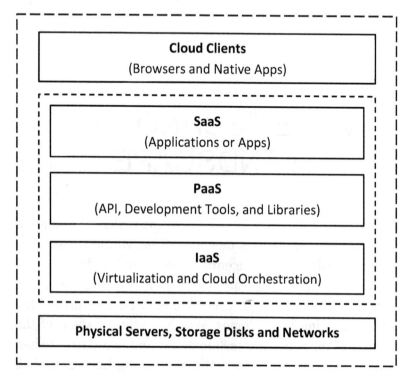

[Figure 4.1: The Cloud Technology Stack]

The stack consists of three layers, creates valued services on the top of the dumb hardware, and delivers these services to users through their cloud clients like web browsers or native applications (Apps) sitting on their devices like desktop, laptop, tablet or smartphone. This may seem to be a long description; but it works as it tells the entire story in a comprehensive way.

We shall start our discussion from bottom to top. The interconnected hardware devices that make the hardware platform serves the basis of infrastructure. We shall not discuss about physical servers, storage disks or network as we assume it to be an obvious thing for IT users. Well, we do not assume any special skills, and shall rather elaborate any specific technical terms in detail if we use it during our discussion.

In fact, IaaS layer consists of a set of software tools, called **cloud toolkits**, which interface with the cloud hardware layer. Let us initiate our discussion by looking at the key concepts like virtualization and cloud orchestration that are part of these toolkits.

Virtualization Is the Key

Virtualization is the buzz-word of today, and is the key constituent in building cloud system. Virtualization refers to creating a virtual version of something, be it server machine, storage container, operating system or even network resource.

In simple terms, hardware virtualization pertains to the task of making hardware platform capable of running multiple copies of OSs or multiple sessions of single OS simultaneously. In this process, each copy of OS is isolated from all other copies in all reasonable terms while adhering to the internal communication guidelines.

What happens to the behavior of OS in such an environment? How different copies interact with one another that will offer a framework for networking within the same environment? How will the applications hosted in such virtual machines behave? What special care will be taken to run these applications successfully? Let us find answers to these questions below.

To understand this, let us do an abstraction of the entire scenario. The hardware platform is dumb without a software component sitting and working on it. This software, popularly called as a **Virtual Machine Manager (VMM) or a hypervisor**, enables the available hardware resources to be fragmented into different virtual machines each being allocated with resources like RAM, processing power, and storage etc. This software controls and manages the VMs. An Operation System (OS) on a VM is treated as a bundle of programs along with their states by this parent software platform. OS in such incarnation can readily be used without going through the process of installations and configurations. On the other hand, these VMs are setup not to allow unwanted traffic from other VMs. In a networking framework, this mimics the traditional world. IPs and subnet masks are allocated to VMs to make the virtualization complete (figure 4.1).

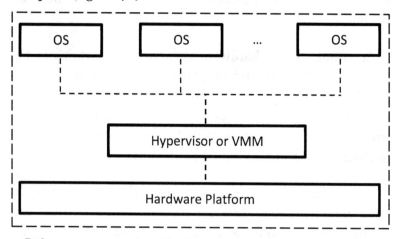

[Figure 4.2: A Simplistic Model of Virtualization]

Well, as we discussed above, we restricted ourselves to virtualization within a single physical machine. On the other hand, grid computing has already given adequate amount of expertise to gather multiple machines to enable a distributed environment for computing. Putting both into a single integrated perspective, we can extend the concept of virtualization across multiple machines spread over multiple geographical locations. And, of course, we add the components like automated tools for provisioning and managing computing resources based on metered usages (many refer to this as 'utility computing' model) to realize a comprehensive picture of cloud computing. Moreover, user applications hosted on such a platform is not aware of these changed details while leveraging all advantages like scalability and redundancy associated with the new platform. Application is open to communicate with one another, and even across different clouds through their APIs adhering to standard protocols like SOAP, ReST, XML-RPC; and in this way, they scale out horizontally. We shall discuss this in detail in a separate section later in this chapter.

Going back to our ongoing discussion, offerings from Oracle, Microsoft, Citrix and VMware are very popular in the segment of virtualization. Respective websites will provide the details of these products along with feature comparisons and other technical details. In fact, all major IT companies are investing significantly in achieving seamless process of virtualization from hardware to application level. The drivers of such effort include the expectations of greater control over the OS and applications hosted within, provisioning and managing applications, middleware and databases, accelerating application deployment, lower cost, scalability, and high availability.

Orchestrating Cloud Infrastructure

Do not confuse this with software stack that will be delivered in PaaS model. Here, we are talking about an integrated management of cloud infrastructure to be delivered in IaaS model. In fact, the concept of virtualization across multiple hardware systems led to the projects for building an integrated cloud platform.

Early efforts can be traced to projects such as Nebula by NASA and Eucalyptus, originated from a research project in the Computer Science Department at the University of California, Santa Barbara. Later Rackspace and NASA collaborated along with a growing list of partners for an open source project called Openstack, which is now in the process of becoming the de facto platform for public and private clouds. Apart from this, there are several other products which have received good acceptance, notable among them is Cloudstack sponsored by Citrix, Flexiscale, which was in fact launched shortly after Amazon's EC2 service, Opennebula, and Skytap.

Each cloud platform offers its own set of terminologies while bringing the conceptual foundation to working. However, all of these adopt a set of broad guidelines and goals:

- Capability to build, manage and deploy IaaS offerings, for example, like Amazon EC2 and S3

- Agnostic to hypervisors, or at least support for all popular hypervisors from different vendors

- Equipped with tools for managing heterogeneous distributed datacenter infrastructures

- An easy-to-use web interface, command line, and a full-featured RESTful API (honoring ReST protocol).

While major cloud vendors have built platforms for IaaS offerings, the architecture and product features are in a rapid process of evolution.

On the other hand, different cloud management tools have been created that can support across multiple vendors and across different deployment models. Prominent players like RightScale, Enstratus, Kaavo, and Scalr provide such solutions in SaaS model – applications that interface with IaaS offerings for easy management and monitoring of cloud resources across different vendors.

As we learnt about cloud orchestration, we must note that it is not just hardware platform or OS that we control, but we also control and manage data storage and network. We shall discuss these two in the next two sections respectively.

Handling Big Data Effectively

We have already discussed about big data in the last chapter. We speak about big data in a scenario where the existing Relational Database Management Systems (RDBMS); and the associated tools are simply inadequate to manage such data. In fact, this signifies a much broader thing than the voluminous data size as indicated previously.

Big data has two qualitative, and three major quantitative, attributes that define it in a comprehensive manner (figure: 4.3).

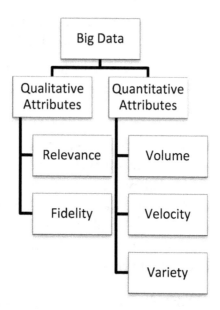

[Figure 4.3: Attributes of Big Data]

The qualitative parameters are **relevance** and **fidelity**. The data must be relevant for the purpose. When we speak of big data, we refer to data that can pile incessantly; and thus the question of relevance becomes so important. For an example, we may accumulate data from a surveillance camera (an example that we had placed in the Chapter 1), but we must store images of requisite resolution for the requisite period of time for creating event based alerts.

Fidelity of data refers to the trust associated with the data. This depends on different parameters like the source of data, and the method of their retrieval or accumulation, and the format.

Other attributes of data that are critical to define big data, are quantitative. The first parameter, volume, has already been discussed, and refers to the large volume of data. In the context of data storage and accessing data for useful analytics, it is required to have faster append and retrieval process in place – the greater velocity of data. The data storage must have interface to be able to meet these requirements like rapid updates on a social networking site or to serve real-time analytics in an enterprise. Finally, the third parameter, variety, refers to the multitude of data formats that we are using these days like graphics, audio, video, texts, documents apart from transactional data (those stored in relational databases).

How to manage big data? If we look across various IT systems in operation today, we can see a mixture of established practices along with some forward looking implementations to manage data at this scale.

RDBMS has been a preferred tool to manage data for last couple of decades. While these database systems like Oracle, MySQL, MS SQL Server, etc. provide a well-structured storage and retrieval system, they come with their overheads due their compliance with **ACID (Atomicity, Consistency, Isolation and Durability) properties**. To manage growing data size and I/O requirements, a few attempts have been made during the course of time like master-slave architecture and **database sharding** (or horizontal partitioning) to achieve a workaround with the existing relational databases. But these options were costly and cumbersome.

As people started looking at the method of data management with a revised perspective, it became important either to give priority to high availability of data or to their consistency. In fact, there emerged the famous theorem by

Eric Brewer, the **CAP theorem**, which postulates that any distributed data system can have only two of three properties like consistency (C), high availability (A), and tolerance to network partitions (P). Though it is not my intention to drag you into a technical discussion about this theorem, it is pertinent to draw your attention to its relevance in the current situation of handling big data. Moreover, quick addition (technically appending data to the existing data store) and retrieval of data removes the need of having a single up-to-date copy of data at any given time, an ACID property. Though this requirement of the consistency of data cannot be ignored altogether, mandatory requirements have gone with the kind of data in question; and a new breed of database management systems, called noSQL (Not Only SQL), have compensated the needs. These database systems are categorized according to the way they store and facilitate access to data:

- **Key-value Stores:** These allow to store data in a schema-less way. There is no need for a fixed data model; rather data could be stored in an object. Major examples are Apache Cassandra and Amazon DynamoDB.

- **BigTable:** It is a high performance and compressed database system by Google. It is currently available with Google AppEngine. However, there are different clones/derivatives of this database that have come into scene in the recent years like HyperTable and LevelDB, etc.

- **Document Store:** This is designed for storing, retrieving, and managing document-oriented, or semi structured data. This type of database is also called a

Document-oriented Database. CouchDB, MongoDB are two examples of this category of databases.

* **Graph Databases:** These use graph structures with nodes, edges, and properties to represent and store data. AllegroGraph, InfoGrid, and Neo4j are a few examples of this type of databases.

It would be a different exercise to learn these databases and to use them; in fact, the exercise can be a whole new book altogether. I would rather offer a brief discussion about them here.

The noSQL databases are still evolving, and are following the experiences gained from handling different systems using big data, and associating different mathematical concepts to solve these problems. The major areas that are driving innovations in these new breed of database systems are social networking, real-time analytics, context-aware computing requirements for mobile users among others. However, it is also clear that these systems adapt and exploit the distributed architecture of cloud to achieve desired performance and scaling; and we shall discuss this in the following section.

Working in Distributed Architecture

All along, we have seen the advantage of scaling horizontally, and the ease and economic feasibility associated with such an endeavor. On the other hand, it is required to understand the architectural differences that exist in such scenarios where the system is spread over multiple devices, perhaps across different geographical locations. The situation becomes engaging when the participating devices have different configurations and possess different software environments. Well, that is what we want to handle when we talk of distributed systems!

We have already discussed the way the hardware platform is scaled, and how we control and manage such infrastructure. However, it is also important to understand the way the user's request is met from the cloud. We must have an understanding of the way requests from user to the source of data, and the flow of data from the source to its destination or user are managed. Please note that we use the term "user" as a synonym of any client, be it a thin client or another application on the cloud.

It is normal to think of HTTP protocol to be responsible for the majority of data transactions over Internet. While, there are other protocols, which can be more convenient for certain situations, HTTP has gained popularity due to its simplicity and ease of use in all situations. Putting along our perspective, this protocol is the carrier for all user requests (HTTP Requests) and all responses from the cloud (HTTP response).

But, how are these requests recognized and how are the cloud resources identified? This is done by **Domain Name Service (DNS)**, a hierarchical naming system of Internet resources. The resources are named after domain names, which can be understood as the human-friendly identifiers to different resources available on Internet for consumption.

While DNS enables identification to resources, the process of redirection of access to a copy of the resource depends on the **Load Balancer**. It regulates the access to a particular resource, and ensures its availability based on geographical proximity, and access to the next nearest neighbor in case of a situation of partition where cycle of a transaction gets disrupted due to unavailability of dependent resources.

[Figure 4.4: Important Components of a Distributed System that Facilitate User Requests and Response from Cloud for Content]

The next thing is to do the actual serving of data to users based on their request. This is done through a **Content Delivery Network (CDN)**, a geographically distributed network setup to increase the availability of resources based on geographical proximity and to reduce the latency of accessing resources. Currently, only large IT infrastructure providers make CDN available. Akamai is the largest CDN provider with 1,00,000 servers spread over 70 countries around the globe. Cloud providers like Amazon and Microsoft also have their own CDNs. Telecommunications service providers offer CDN services to reduce demand on their network resources and to leverage costs of their huge infrastructures.

In fact, we are participating in a rapidly evolving Internet ecosystem. Streaming rich media (disseminating audio and video over Internet to achieve a steady flow of data at the client devices) has pushed the boundary of how we shall deal with content, and has led into **mass customerization** of content publishing and consumption.

All these happen due to innovations on the side of datacenters that ensure sustainable and better delivery of applications and content. Let us now turn our attention to discuss it in detail.

Datacenters See Transformations

As chip technologies are evolving with active participation from industry, and newer possibilities are emerging with applications of photonics and nanotechnology, the server hardware, storage and network devices are seeing rapid changes. Apart from just items, which are directly associated with capital expenditures, vendors are in constant process of innovation to optimize energy efficiency at datacenters and automation of various processes therein. In fact, cost of power and cooling infrastructure can equal, or even exceed, the cost of IT hardware in a datacenter. Thus adopting cheaper energy sources, cooling mechanisms along with newer tools, and improved process of managing energy utilization will help. Some guidelines in this regard are:

- Ensuring infrastructure design for optimum performance and availability throughout its life-cycle

- Integration of service demands with the supply of resources for efficient scheduling of resources

- Monitoring services in association with usages and quality to determine sustainability and continual improvements

- Ensuring high availability of resources in situations of partition

It is also imperative to correlate cloud services with optimal, yet sustainable, resource management to take appropriate business decision to reduce the overall cost of service delivery while providing a sustainable solution. On the other hand, the evolution is not one-sided; i.e., we also see rapid changes to the technologies used at the consumer-side. Let us discuss these in the following section.

New Devices, New Ways to Use

The changing lifestyle and usage of different electronic gadgets have influenced the way we manage our information and content. Innovations have greatly supported the changed behavior largely in sync with the expectations from end-users.

If we track news in IT or the new gadget section in any RSS feed, we come across new devices almost daily (we have happily adopted these new ways of information consumption going away from the traditional news magazines; if you have not done yet, it's worth trying!). The look of devices, their sizes, and the utilities available within are seeing a sea-change. As we have discussed the concept of 'universal access' in Chapter 3, people would like to access different devices as it suits their usage patterns while being connected to all of their data. These demands have given rise to requirements like standardization of software platform, user settings, applications for accessing data, and above all, interoperability of data across various user devices.

Defining an App – A New Incarnation

As we discussed about cloud technology stack, we could see that it was broadly the handiwork of some software that leverages the power of hardware to render cloud services. Moreover, in any normal situation, multiple software applications work in unison to help a service materialize.

This gives rise to a new incarnation of software, the way we view and use it.

"Anything can be an App" is the key to conceive how software is being made and used. An App may be defined as an self-sustainable software entity which can be used alone or with other Apps to create a software service.

[Figure 4.5: Components of an App]

Each App has a few important characteristics that define it and provide a broad picture of its architecture and usages. We shall discuss six major characteristics below:

- **Business Operations:** When we talk of an App, we expect that it must achieve certain thing(s) when requested, and must be able to provide us requisite data in the desired form. The computing processes that ensue after the request is received are broadly termed as business operations. In fact, there can be multiple operations possible depending on the complexities and goals. These processes can be classified into three categories such as the processes of updates and retrievals, that of interfacing with I/O devices, and that of managing resource allocation and release. Business operations achieve the specific requirements that the App is meant for.

- **Disconnected Operations:** There can be a situation when one or more resources within an App fail to execute. This situation is called a 'partition' as we know by now. It is a critical parameter in cloud scenario as the resources are distributed across many devices and different geographical locations (I believe you will find our earlier discussion on CAP theorem more relevant in this context). The user device is also considered to be a part of it. People call a partition as an 'offline mode' if the connectivity of the user device is lost from the remote cloud system. We are familiar with offline mode while using Apps like Google Mail and Docs, etc. In such cases, an offline component of App is also available natively on the user device along with a copy of data (may not be an updated one). When there is no internet connectivity, you are still using almost the full application except that the updates we perform may be delayed from being synchronized with the cloud system until the connectivity is restored. These delayed updates and the synchronization of data get complex when activities like access from different devices are involved. At present, the native clients built with HTML5 do support local storage, and are capable of managing offline mode in spite of certain inherent limitations. Thus various techniques that are in use to handle disconnected operations will have to mature. In fact, these mechanisms are still evolving, and are in active development.

- **Metadata:** An App must be identified uniquely to be used by other Apps to complete requisite business operations. The usual process of locating an App would be to look up a database of Apps based on appropriate criteria. This will be possible if each App will have appropriate description, taxonomic data associated with it. These data are termed as metadata, and include a unique ID (using domain name system as universal identifier) apart from others.

- **API (Application Programming Interface):** As we discussed about involving multiple Apps to achieve any normal IT computing task, it is required that Apps must work in unison, and should be able to exchange data with one another seamlessly. For this, each App must be able to understand the data exchange protocols, accept data format of another, and respond in a manner that the recipient App can understand. Currently, ReST, SOAP and XML-RPC are being used commonly as data exchange protocols whereas ReST is the most popular one due to its ease of use. Similarly, standard formats like XML and JSON are being used popularly as data exchange formats though the latter has an edge as JavaScript is being used dominantly on cloud clients.

- **Identity Management:** When an App accesses another App, the first responsibility lies in validating the identity of the request, and confirming if it complies to the requisite access privileges. There are different protocols like **OpenID** and **oAuth** that are used to make this process easy. These encourage accessing applications across different ecosystems without creating separate identity for each one, a popular model called **Single Sign-On (SSO)**. The other part of the data access after validating the identity is the access control over resources based on pre-assigned privileges to client. Role-Based Access Control (RBAC) schemes are the most popular ones. If you scan the research literatures, you will see a number of derivatives that have been proposed, and are being used as appropriate in different scenarios. Broadly these schemes define the regulation in access control based on user roles rather than the users themselves.

- **SLA:** In normal business situations, SLAs (Service Level Agreements) are used to create a legal document to ensure correct delivery of services along with clear guidelines for actions in case of failures in conforming to the agreement. In similar fashion, SLA is also needed at the App-level that must include the allowed and denied resources, protocols and requests.

Now, we can perceive an App as something which delivers IT resources directly to its valid user, or to another intermediate App through standard protocols and in standard data exchange formats. Apps mask the details of the business operations from all others except providing a standard interface, API, and ensure the data access in a secured manner.

Broad Classification of Apps

Many would not agree to a particular way of classifying Apps. In fact, there are different ways which we can use to classify Apps like kind of industry they are serving, and the type of devices they interact with, etc. However, we shall adopt an approach based on the kind of business operations an App executes (figure 4.6). This approach will adhere to the technology stack closely, and will provide us an insight into the working of Apps in different scenarios.

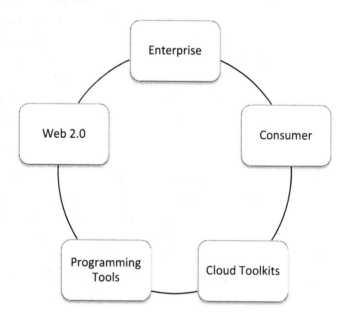

[Figure 4.6: Different Types of Apps]

While we discussed IaaS layer of the Cloud Technology Stack, we talked about the cloud toolkits that are responsible for providing a high-level and usable interface to the hardware platform on cloud. These toolkits are in the state of rapid evolution; and the major thrust is now on more control and auto-management.

Programming Tools are basically associated with the next layer in the stack, PaaS. These include frameworks, application builders, programming libraries, and API suites, etc. These tools mostly focus on specific programming languages and technologies.

Other three categories of Apps pertain to the SaaS layer in the stack. These Apps may have a native counterpart sitting on user devices. A major category in this layer is Web 2.0 Apps, which are used for social networking sites, e-commerce storefronts, and knowledge management portals among others. An important thrust in such Apps is on managing crowd-sourced content; technically, on the process of rapid append and retrieval.

In contrast, the Enterprise Apps emphasize on transactional data management procedures; and these Apps are used in different mission-critical scenarios of business, government and research. These Apps can serve across multiple industry verticals. For example, the backend of a storefront is managed through these kind of Apps, which achieve successful transactions without fuss.

Finally, the Consumer Apps, are the ones which are meant for individual users for their personal needs. With the proliferation of devices, and increasing dependence of lifestyle utilities, this kind of Apps has a significant market-size. Location-based and context-aware technologies such as triggering an action based on location and context are predominant in these Apps.

With a discussion about different Apps on cloud, let us now look at the generic cloud scenario, how Apps behave in a collective environment, and what we expect from them. This is what we shall discuss in the following section.

A Federated Ecosystem

Can we think of a solitary App meeting all our requirements? No, rather we deal with a set of Apps that work together to achieve a real-world task. Each App gets engaged in multi-point interactions among the group of Apps to deliver desired services while maintaining the requisite isolation and independent operations within themselves. This is a truly a federated ecosystem where Apps interact with one another in a disciplined fashion adhering to standard protocols and data exchange formats. Figure 4.7 illustrates different properties of an App that are important to account for in this federated structure.

The most important activity before interacting with any App is to find it. It is required that an App must be available in a search database with necessary information (metadata of App). The discovery of an App by others must be made automatic if we have to obey the cloud characteristics.

After an App is discovered, the next important activity is to validate the requested requirements and available facility through an automatic App-level SLA. Then billing terms must also have to be adhered to if it is a requirement of the SLA; of course, all at App-level. In fact, different vendors are now equipping their devices with billing capability, in turn the Apps installed in those devices. Also, different Apps are getting bundled with the capability to manage billing through their user identities; and Google Wallet to Android Apps point at the evolution in this direction.

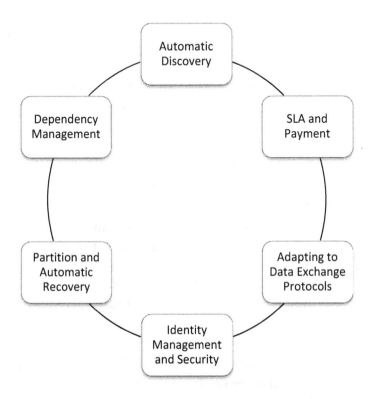

[Figure 4.7: Group Behavior of Apps in a Federated Ecosystem]

We shall go to next activity after contract is made between two Apps for their proposed data transactions. However, we know that data exchanges must abide by one of the standard protocols; and the data format has to be in one of the standard formats. Moreover, both the interacting Apps must obey the same protocol, and exchange data in the same format to facilitate successful interaction; but this may not be possible looking at the multiple popular protocols and data exchange formats. Thus it may be required to come up with a single standard protocol and to adopt a single standard data exchange format between Apps. The other option would be to inject necessary capability to Apps to adapt to different standard protocols and formats.

When we talk of a **live App**, we refer to an instance of an App run by a user or a virtual agent embedded in another App. And, it becomes quite important for the live App to manage the identity of the request, and to provide only those privileges that the request is authorized for. We have already discussed this aspect of identity management and security in detail in the previous section. We would rather limit our discussion here by stating that each live App must have a user role associated with it to make a request to another App.

Well, we just discussed the interaction mechanisms for Apps and different aspects involved. On the other hand, the major issue that is rather more relevant in the cloud environment is the situation of partition. Such a situation always hinders successful interactions between Apps, and results in unfulfilled requests. When we need to accept the situation of partition as a reality, we must also have the Apps to recover from the state of partition automatically. The automatic recovery manages the processes like delayed updates and synchronization of data through self-audit and control mechanisms. In fact, the situation turns complex when there are dependencies between Apps for one successful transaction at the user-end, and when a state of partition occurs. In such cases, the application must be able to determine its dependency, auto-restart the process of recovery (auto-recovery), and inform the end-user with suitable feedbacks during the process.

New Solution to the Old Problem

In this chapter, we reviewed the technologies associated with cloud computing paradigm, and analyzed the technology scenario at an abstraction of Cloud Technology Stack. Through the entire discussion, we could see the changing nature of software and a new definition of an App. This change in approach creates an abundant opportunities for new solutions.

In the following chapter, we shall look at the old problem of implementing IT, and the migration of existing systems to meet the newer challenges.

5 DOING BUSINESS ON CLOUD

As the adoption of cloud solutions are on a steady increase across verticals and businesses of different sizes, the supply-chain and possibility of innovations have generated multitude of business opportunities. Demands from business users drive innovations on the side of providers. In this chapter, we shall analyze the background for the change in business processes, and ways to implement IT and migrate existing systems in this changing scenario. We shall also review different possible business models based on cloud computing. We shall make effort to cover various practical aspects or examples during our discussion.

Things Are Changing

There have been many changes in the way we do business in present times though we are oblivious of use of the technologies working behind it. Let us discuss some of the major changes that are directly related to cloud computing.

It is quite difficult to cover all areas that have seen influences of this computing paradigm; in fact, almost all have already. However, we shall discuss only some of the widespread impacts on business processes that rely heavily on collaboration and on online media, and the changes in the way SMEs (Small and Medium Enterprises) operate.

After creation, editing and sharing of online documents have been possible through cloud-based Apps, things have drastically changed the way we store data and collaborate with others. Though skeptics complain about security aspects, the ease of doing our jobs overshadowed such concerns. Currently, people collaborate at various levels using textual data, documents, audio and video; and use cloud Apps to manage their workflows with workforce spread across different geographical locations. Let us look at an example.

When you want a logo for your company to be created, you can post your requirements on a website for such specialized service. Different professionals around the globe participate in the bidding; and you get the best possible product at an appropriate price. The service provider who facilitates such infrastructure uses cloud computing to manage data and programs at an Internet scale.

In fact, we can go on providing such interesting examples. In each case, however, cloud computing works to materialize the computation requirements.

Let us look at the publishing industry. Gone are those days when you write a book, create music compositions, or produce a documentary film, and then wait for a publisher or a distributor to accept it. Different independent publishing tools are provided by various service providers on cloud which enable your creative product to materialize into a finished one and to be promoted in public domain. Google and Amazon among others have pioneered in such publishing effort. The number of books that are being published has increased by many folds in recent years; and the approach to publishing books and magazines have transformed greatly (http://www.time.com/time/magazine/article/0,9171,1873122,00.html).

Moreover, the process of publishing news and articles has gone through a complete transformation in recent years. Freelance journalists and companies providing online news services make their content available for free subscription or with a minimal subscription fee, making the print newspapers almost obsolete as days go by. In fact, live streaming and offering valued content on Internet have created a strong proposition to integrate the two media. What is the common thing behind success of all these new business opportunities? It's cloud computing.

Of course, these are not solitary happenings. Each industry is sensing the change in business processes and creating new business models through this new technology paradigm. However, the major beneficiaries are SMEs, where upfront investment in IT may be considered as a burden, yet challenges in business demands higher level of productivity and decision-making.

On the other hand, the number of SMEs is increasing rapidly across the globe; and they are responsible for a significant portion of business transactions, and above all, for sustainability of economy in general. These enterprises adopt cloud computing faster. In fact, new generation entrepreneurs in service industry use cloud computing to their advantage when they test their novel ideas in market while avoiding large expenses or seeking investments from others. A win-win situation.

As we see a change that is pervasive, let us review different aspects of successful cloud adoption in the following section.

Behind Successful Adoption of Cloud

Business is not a contemporary word. It is a part and parcel of the entire human history. As human society has evolved, the ways of doing business has also changed. Human has adopted new models that suit the interest groups, and also, that keep the economic momentum up. We can look at the adoption of cloud computing in business from the same perspective; in fact, our conviction is well founded when we recollect our discussion regarding the growth in cloud adoption (Chapter 3).

We can now understand that three major factors that influence successful adoption of new technologies, are overall cost, quality of service and business agility (figure: 5.1). The same is true for cloud computing. In fact, recollecting our previous discussion in Chapter 3, we can very well say that the adoption of cloud computing is not uniform across enterprises even within the same industry verticals. The path of adoption varies based on the state of IT in the enterprise and their business goals.

Business agility requires how an enterprise would respond to changes, and how IT, as the critical business enabler, adapts to such changes.

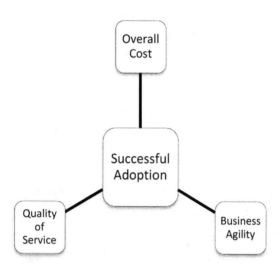

**[Figure 5.1: Factors That Drive Successful Adoption
of Cloud Computing]**

The above discussion is generic, and must be applied with measurable parameters in all practical purposes to achieve successful adoption. Moreover, additional criteria come into picture when we select different service levels and different deployment scenarios while adopting cloud implementation for your IT.

Selection of service model while adopting cloud is a business decision based on the core capability of the adopter. For example, a business running on cloud will choose SaaS over others as they prefer to quickly reap the benefit of going cloud. Similarly, selection of public versus private cloud depends on different criteria. IDC has prescribed five factors that greatly influence the decision to adopt public versus private clouds such as specific needs of application, service level guarantees, security/access/data ownership, total cost of hardware and total cost of software licenses (figure 5.2).

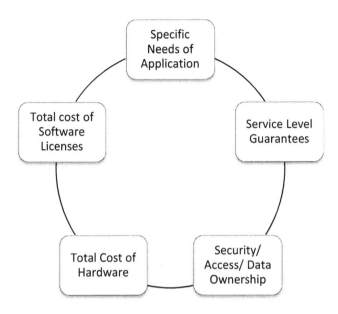

[Figure 5.2: Factors Determining Adoption of Public versus Private Cloud (Source: IDC)]

While we have a fair knowledge of the factors behind the successful adoption of cloud, we need to understand the scenarios in which it is adopted. This is the topic of the next section.

Cloud Adoption Scenarios

Cloud computing paradigm has its advantage in its usage. In fact, the real benefits have been incorporated into the paradigm itself. Apart from general advantages that we have seen during the earlier discussion, it is pertinent to view the possibility of usage in specific scenarios.

If we scan through different areas of usages, we shall find numerous ways for its successful adoption and gaining significant advantage. However, to make our study comprehensive and systematic, let us classify the available scenarios into five broad categories (figure 5.3).

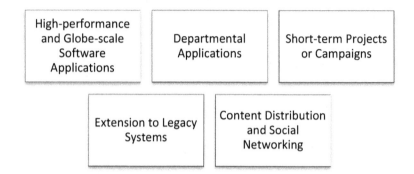

[Figure 5.3: Different Cloud Adoption Scenarios]

Let us now understand these five different scenarios for adoption of cloud computing:

1. **High-performance and Globe-scale Software Applications:** When people require large-scale computing where performance or availability under high-traffic situation is critical, cloud solution is preferred. It is also pertinent to note that the choice of service model is a different thing to consider, and is not at all related to the parameters under consideration.

2. **Departmental Applications:** Even though standard applications take care of the major data management needs, people in various departments in an enterprise do use simple software tools like MS Office, Open Office or similar ones. They use these to create plans, discuss strategy, and create various reports, even with the data retrieved from central data

repository of the company. In such situations, departments opt for software applications to be used on SaaS model as that can be launched without much involvement of IT department and availability is far better compared to the traditional solutions that we mentioned. Of course, a hybrid model of using traditional software along with cloud services may suit as the latter provides rich interface for exploiting available features for work needs while the former provides high availability and facilitates greater collaboration.

3. **Short-term Projects or Campaigns:** Organizations go on marketing campaigns or adopt a short-term collaboration for different project needs. In such cases, company does not want to invest upfront as the return on investment (ROI) is not known beforehand, at times. It may also be true that there is no scope of allowing a period of latency to initiate such activity. Both situations provide excellent cases to substantiate our previous preaching of reducing TCO and TTV, as discussed in Chapter 3; and cloud computing remains the best possible option here.

4. **Extension to Legacy Systems:** Companies have already invested their fortune into building their IT systems through past couple of decades. While these systems are still reliable and are capable of managing the mainstream tasks, user needs have increased through the years. While full migration to newer system and abandoning the older system are costly propositions, using extensions of these legacy systems on cloud enables greater availability of data, and

79

better collaboration. It also helps us use enterprise data to make rightful decisions based on analytics, and adopt newer applications into the existing enterprise IT ecosystem.

5. **Content Distribution and Social Networking:** With newer possibilities of publishing, relationship management and marketing, content (both in form of text and rich media) is exploding in size. With self-publishing promoted by cloud providers like Amazon.com and Lulu.com apart from others, and popularity of social media like Facebook and YouTube among others, the creation and use of content have seen a sea change in recent times. These cloud systems provide federated ecosystems that facilitate building new apps and new revenue generation models among users. Apart from popular notion of individual affinity towards such clouds, business entities are also investing on linking their systems with these cloud systems for effective online promotions and for gathering competitive business intelligence.

Though we discussed some of the most important adoption scenarios, you will not be surprised if somebody comes up with another tomorrow. In fact, there are multitude usages that cloud computing has encouraged; and possibilities are many.

Factors Influencing Cloud Adoption

Talking about going cloud without knowing about different factors that influence the adoption would be a mistake. We need to understand the general issues that we would encounter during and after the process of migration, and should have reasonable solution planned beforehand.

Shifting our personal IT to cloud may not be difficult as this will mostly involve data porting while remaining items will be within the purview of decision-making of the individual. However, the situation is not so simple when we look at the enterprise systems. In such cases, we also need to understand and account for all relevant factors influencing a successful cloud adoption.

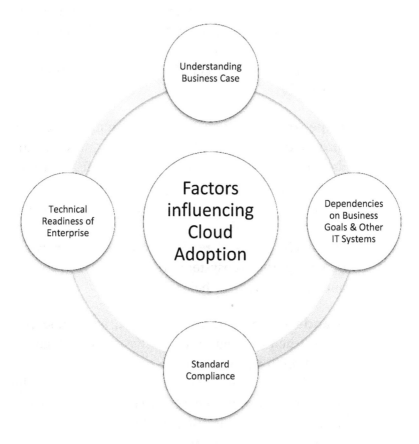

[Figure 5.4: Factors Influencing Cloud Adoption]

These issues are broadly classified into four categories as in figure 5.4. Let us discuss these towards a successful cloud adoption below:

1. **Understanding the Business Case:** It is quite normal that strategic and operational requirements in enterprises differ from one another across different verticals and even within the same vertical. Though it is not apparent when we look at these in broad terms, devils are in detail. As the part of the migration strategy, it is required that we understand what the exact needs are, which are not fulfilled with the existing IT framework, and which are the clear advantages that we get if we go cloud entirely or selectively.

2. **Dependencies on Different Business Goals and Other IT Systems:** Before making any decision for adopting cloud services for the entire IT or for partial use, we must evaluate the dependencies among the existing systems within the enterprise and also those operating immediately along the supply-chain. The issues of retaining the consistency while operating each subsystem after migration is crucial, and must be resolved beforehand.

3. **Standard Compliance:** This is a very important factor when we migrate to any newer system, and is more prominent when we use public cloud in part or fully for our solutions. We have cherished the discussion on requirements of standard compliance of Apps in the last chapter, and the sense of validity persists in case of adopting cloud solution (please

note that the phrases such as solution and service are interchangeable here).

4. **Technical Readiness of Enterprise:** Skills of users, their access conditions, and the purpose of usage determine which solutions would be appropriate and the path we should take for achieving a successful adoption. While migrating to cloud environment, it is important to study the readiness of enterprise before making a move.

The above discussion provides broad guidelines for implementing IT by adopting cloud computing, either partially or fully. However, it is essential that we must have adequate planning and proper execution of the plan to achieve success. The entire process needs to be executed with diligence; and we shall talk about this in the next section.

Create Your Cloud Strategy

In general, the basic cloud IT strategy requires a well-defined path from planning to implementation and evaluation (figure 5.5).

The process starts with a plan to implement a new IT system or to migrate an existing one. As usual, architecture is important, and that needs to be taken care of. Based on architecture, the system implementation needs to be carried out. The new system must be sustainable for a reasonable period. This provides us scope to pursue innovations in different fronts. We need to evaluate the entire system, innovations, and their impact comprehensively. In case of migration, the revision to the existing architecture and its impact must be evaluated. This, in fact, completes a cycle and the same new cycle then repeats.

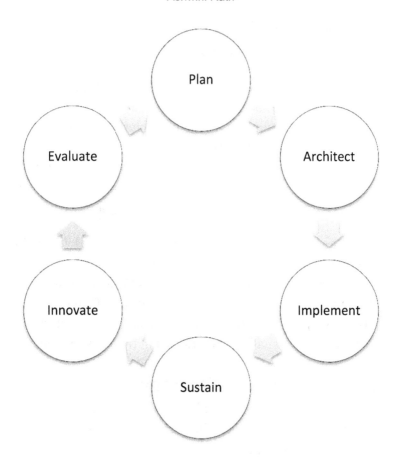

[Figure 5.5: Cloud IT Strategy]

On the other hand, we must take into account the adoption scenario and the factors influencing a successful adoption in detail during the planning and execution.

Emergence of a Federated Business Ecosystem

If we look at the cloud ecosystem, we can notice different stakeholders responsible for playing different roles along the entire supply-chain. This chain usually span over multiple organizations having different core objectives, independent operations and management processes. However, they interact among one another drawing inspiration from the concept of Apps that we discussed in Chapter 4; and make a federated ecosystem.

For example, a service provider with IaaS will depend on developers, on one hand, to create new cloud toolkit or to upgrade the existing ones. On the other hand, the same provider will depend on other providers with PaaS to offer value-added services on the top of the available infrastructure. It may also be possible for the developers to subscribe to the infrastructure services to test and to deploy their Apps. It is a synergetic relationship.

The way the interactions between different stakeholders of a cloud ecosystem happen, we can visualize a federated conglomeration of different businesses and end-users.

Different Service Providers Coexist

We shall now review different types of Cloud Service Providers. In figure 5.6, a broad classification of different service providers associated with cloud computing ecosystems are presented.

Cloud Infrastructure Service Providers (CISP) are the ones who provide IaaS. These are major players in the industry who can invest significantly in creating large-scale infrastructure and maintaining it. The major players in this segment are Rackspace and Amazon, etc. Similarly, Cloud Platform Service Providers (CPSP) offer PaaS. They provide programming tools and facility for building and deploying applications faster and with ease. Google and Microsoft are two major players in this segment.

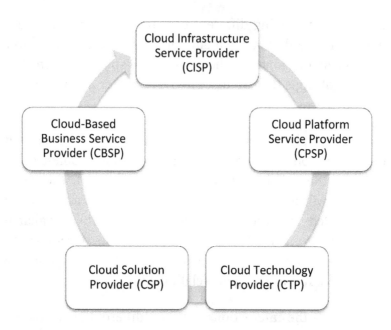

[Figure 5.6: Different Business Models]

Next, Cloud Technology Providers (CTP) create and supply technology tools and products to different cloud service providers. Similarly, Cloud Solution Providers (CSP) provide different IT solutions based on infrastructure and platform services. SaaS providers are included in this category. Finally, Cloud-based Business Service Providers (CBSP) are the ones who provide various services that depend primarily on cloud technologies.

Let us now see in the next section how the transition of existing roles has taken place in this changed scenario.

Old Players with New Roles

With cloud computing gaining ground in different sectors, existing IT roles are receiving new demands. The responsibilities of these roles have also seen changes apart from just their names.

We can see major roles that have been visible these days (figure 5.7) such as Cloud Administrator (CA), cloud Developer (CD), Cloud Service Manager (CSM), Cloud App Architect (CAA), and Cloud User (CU).

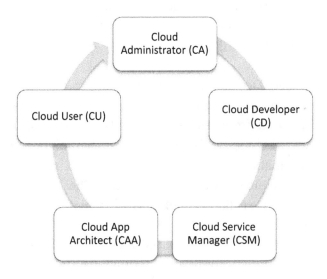

[Figure 5.7: Different Roles for IT Professionals While Working in Cloud Environment]

Let us now discuss each of these roles played by IT professionals in detail below:

- **Cloud Administrator (CA):** The role of old System Administrator has seen changes during the course of time. With the GUI tools being available, some of the responsibilities are being passed to service managers. On the other hand, system administrators are being asked to perform complex task of managing the backend tools and subsystems. The earlier role had the responsibilities like managing the servers, networking, installing and managing storage arrays, load balancers, DSN, etc. These activities have been eased considerably due to the availability of APIs to manage these; and Administrators have migrated to the backend of cloud environment leaving earlier responsibilities to Cloud Service Managers (to be discussed later in this section). These require further specialized skills.

- **Cloud Developer (CD):** Developers have got a new role to play in creating new tools and frameworks for cloud environment. As the "self-service" motto is the key behind this computing paradigm, system automation demands greater skills and innovations in the technology development areas. These people many a time are called **Cloud Toolkit Developers**.

- **Cloud Service Manager (CSM):** As more and more organizations adopt cloud computing as their mainstay IT, professionals with knowledge of specific cloud systems are needed in large numbers. These professionals, CSMs, are responsible to provision, monitor and control cloud services on behalf of their clients or the stakeholders.

- **Cloud App Architect (CAA):** Every other day, we see new Apps flooding into Apps stores or market places. This is due to innovative applications of IT for different user expectations and requirements. CAA is an evolution of the traditional software architect, but with changed responsibility where the focus is more on using various services to create new innovative applications.

- **Cloud User (CU):** He/she is anybody who uses Apps on cloud. Though it is currently a separate role, but it may be merged with any IT user's role as cloud adoption becomes ubiquitous.

We have now learnt about different roles within cloud ecosystem though you can find derivatives and many added ones in literatures; but the essence remains unaffected.

Perspective from Traditional IT Users

As we talk about doing business on cloud, things have changed compared to the traditional IT, and the work process associated with it thereby triggering migration to new tools and technologies. In this section we shall try to understand how it looks when traditional IT users venture into the cloud world – with an ambition to leverage this new paradigm for their own benefits.

Cloud system invariably demands 'broad network access', which means consistent internet connectivity (can be also private network connectivity, but let us go by general perception as nothing changes as far as our discussion goes) is required to access remote IT resources from our own devices. Through the technical review in Chapter 4, we now know that the best available way to access these cloud resources is through Apps.

Well, let us try to analyze a traditional IT environment, and look at the changes from the perspective of an IT user.

Previously, a remote IT resource could also be accessed over network, and there are software applications, which were being used to control and manage these resources. Nothing has changed really!

Next, if you have used any popular hosting environment, you must have been familiar with control panels like CPanel, Plesk, etc., which enable common users without much of system administration capability to access and manage the remote server resources. What do these cloud platforms do? The same thing. Of course, there has been a consistent effort to enhance the tools and to make those usable so that common users can leverage the benefits without added technical skills.

Two of the most important objectives of accessing remote server resources are to manage databases and to deploy user-facing software applications. Not much has changed from user perspective as there are tools from the same cloud provider or from 3rd parties to manage such activities. For example, popular tools like Rightscale or Scalr are used to manage different cloud infrastructures like Rackspace and Amazon among others. Well, they also make the same popular tools that are used to achieve database management; thus, 'going cloud' does not require a significant learning curve. Moreover, the tools like load-balancer and redundant DNS management appear here too except that they are encapsulated as Apps and are exposed with APIs to get managed through other Apps.

Basically, we see a smooth transition for traditional IT users as far as the tools and their management are concerned. However, we must not overlook the issues and factors that critically influence the migration of a traditional

IT system to cloud; and we have already discussed this in detail earlier in this chapter.

Competition Turns into Collaboration – Industry Innovates

We have reached a point of time where the competition has been replaced with collaboration. Remember the discourse earlier in this chapter, and also in the last about federated nature of Apps and business, latter deriving the strength from the former.

Well, subscribing to 3rd party services to build your desired App faster, and doing content syndication to avail the contextual information as we like, are two most prominent ways of collaboration today. In fact, this change in our approach within the business purview has generated many opportunities for carrying out innovations as stakeholders of cloud ecosystem can now focus on their core skills better – industry innovates faster than before.

In the next chapter, we shall turn our attention from business and shall focus on the influence of cloud computing on human behavior and the collective behavior of individuals in society.

6 CLOUD COMPUTING AND SOCIETY

In earlier chapters, we have discussed about automobile and IT industries along with different examples on how cloud technologies have influenced not only business and organizations to bring in cardinal changes in their operations and strategies, but also people in their personal lives. These discussions have been intentional from two perspectives. These represent the fact that it is not just IT, but other technologies have also influenced the way we behave and build our social characters. On the other side, we emphasize that IT is ubiquitous in our personal and social lives too; and thus we need to understand the phenomenon better.

Cloud computing has brought IT to common people due to its propositions of cost and universal access, and has attracted popular attention as it enables us to manage and use big data seamlessly. This has almost translated our discussion on general IT into that on cloud computing.

A Digital Way of Life

Widespread usage of social networking in our daily lives has become quite common in present times. People use websites like Facebook, Twitter and Google, etc. to spread their opinions. The tools, available online such as 'like', 'follow', or '+1' on these websites respectively, help people expand their network that has multiplying effects. For example, political campaigns during 'Arab Spring' could not have gathered such popular support without these social networking websites. In fact, celebrities and political leaders use these websites to give their opinion and to garner support from public. Non-profits and charity organizations use these for raising fund, and to create awareness about social causes they vouch for. Researchers, teachers and students use these platforms to network with others having similar interests, and to share ideas and knowledge. In fact, the possibility of sharing an independent unit of information with barely a hundred plus characters has been realized through social networks and SMS – a realization that is powered by cloud computing.

The major change in our behavior can be understood in the way we express ourselves and about our surroundings. We no longer maintain physical albums, nor do we select the 'best' photos due to scarcity of space in the album. We have gone cloud with our albums residing online and securely; and we decide which ones to share within our family and friends, which ones with our co-workers, which ones in public, and which ones to view privately ourselves. We do not get tired of capturing most of life in stills or in videos, and archive those for later.

We no longer keep a nice looking diary in our briefcase; in fact, the items we used to carry for personal information management have either become obsolete or have found their replacements. In the process of change, we do not even carry the same device containing our data as we move. Rather we change our gadgets as per our lifestyle, that too even during a single day, if its suits; but manage our contacts, daily journals, financial details, etc. from cloud. We even manage all our spending online using banking Apps and virtual wallets.

Our ways of spending leisure have changed. We may spend our time by playing some interesting games on cloud solo or by accepting an available partner. Even, we can utilize time in a productive way by working through an e-learning lesson or by discussing with other learners on a difficult topic.

We have changed the way we travel, dine and stay. We depend on location-based Apps to evaluate and decide on available transportation services, restaurants and hotels. We also react immediately from the same location with our opinions about the services, and our surroundings; and publish photos and videos to make the stuff more engaging and real. Yes, our life has changed; we lead a digital way of life.

Our new way of life is giving way to a new social order, and a changed social life. Let us discuss these further in the following sections.

It's a Collective Phenomenon

I would like to draw your attention to the way termites build their mounds. It may look a bit off-the-place; but I am sure that you will realize the importance of bringing it into our discussion.

Termites are small, yet great creatures when we evaluate their individual capabilities against their collective achievement of building large-scale, complex and high-quality living spaces. In fact, they have been so inspiring to us that we have started making effort to replicate their way in creating our own buildings, a branch called **Biomimetics**, mimicking biological systems for the design and engineering of materials and machines.

Well, so much story for now. Why are we talking about this here? It is about the democratic way a group of millions of these creatures work in unison to build their edifices. With downward trends in the cost of digital gadgets, network bandwidth and IT (cloud) services, more and more people are joining the ongoing digital revolution in a big way. Rapid proliferation of self-publishing, sharing of content, and 360-degree participation in online sphere from personal affairs to politics and entertainment to academics, have truly adhered to democratic principles. The acceptance of an opinion, a product, or a personality takes a route that is an illustration of a true collective phenomenon.

No doubt, you would find some negative elements in this ecosystem as elsewhere. But it will not be prudent to moderate the process from one single authority; rather the moderation must come from leaders in respective groups, or perhaps, by drawing consensus among the participating members. Of course, the process of moderation will evolve through sustained negotiations between societies and governments across the globe, and by improving the technologies to monitor and regulate the process without affecting the freedom of individuals and the collective aspirations.

Pressing for Faster Governance

As we have seen the trend in Chapter 3, the spending by governments on cloud computing is on rise. It is not only the developed nations, all governments across the globe have shown their keen interest to implement e-governance, e-health, e-education, knowledge management, and supply-chain management networks, etc. The success of these at the desired scales and costs can only be possible through cloud computing.

A comprehensive discussion about e-governance and related activities will require a whole new book, and we shall certainly avoid discussing here. We would rather focus on the added privileges that are facilitated due to the use of cloud computing in such large common-people-facing processes.

Ideally, adoption of cloud computing provides a level-playing field to developing countries with reference to the developed ones due to cost-advantages. Moreover, cloud computing eliminates the major disadvantages of low-accessibility and higher cost involved in the decentralization of IT infrastructures in under-developed areas, deployment of new software applications, or their seamless upgrades.

Another major application of cloud computing is the storage and usage of data about citizens of respective countries across the globe. Due to increasing security concerns and intention of availing civil benefits to their populace, governments of different countries have implemented or are in the process of implementing biometric identification of their people. These efforts are meant for storing biometric data about the concerned individuals, which include fingerprints, photo of face and iris, etc., apart from demographic information. These are, of course, sensitive data; and security and accuracy of such data are critical for successful implementation of such schemes.

With government getting closer to its citizens with services becoming quicker and transparent, corruptions and bureaucratic delays are expected to be reduced to a great extent. In fact, government will get opinions and support from citizens directly, and will be able to decide on better governance. In fact, the stakeholders in a democracy can move to the next level of collaboration – knowledge sharing and management instead of struggling through bureaucratic hassles and approvals. This would empower individual citizens with adequate information and capabilities to participate in nation-building in a greater way, and would pave the way for strengthening the democratic systems.

Nationalism versus Globalization

Cloud computing has enabled Internet-scale websites facilitating broader collaborations that transcend the national barriers. In fact, a normal person using emails and social networking websites may end up spending more time knowing about news on events across the globe, and interacting with people who may stay elsewhere in the world rather than local events and local people. If we look the trending topics online and people participating for a cause, we can see a supranational pattern gaining ground. People from one part of the globe may get interested in a cause of people living in another part; and this has become an usual phenomenon.

Speaking on nationalism and globalization is not simple. Political, socio-economic considerations are paramount while discussing on such topics. However, we must admit that greater sharing of information and collaborations will enable the whole world to migrate from a strict national framework into a federated ecosystem of interdependent nations.

Agree to Disagree

In present times, the increasing load of information continually challenges our collective imagination. In fact, this phenomenon has the capability to inflict radical changes to our economy and society. Even a small event can have viral effects due to the fast-paced processes of information dissemination, and may result in unexpected situations. Good or bad – it can only be ascertained after its realization.

Though it would be premature to predict the consequence of this rapidly changing worldview, it would be rather wise to have a requisite amount of tolerance to diverse opinions and beliefs. Taking cue from our earlier discussion, we must be aware that our participation in this larger collective phenomenon also brings certain amount of responsibility and accountability.

7 AN OPEN FRONTIER

The skeptics of this new paradigm of computing sometimes trivialize by terming it as the old wine in a new bottle. After such a healthy discussion through the last six chapters, it may be enraging or disappointing. However, I shall argue differently. If a person could draw the popular attention and could increase the adoption of an old brand of wine substantially, I would call it an innovation! On a serious note, we must recognize the significant changes that have occurred not only in our approach to computing in solving social and business problems, but also helped underlying technologies and methods to reshape and evolve during the past few years.

We are now aware that cloud computing offers distinct advantages apart from just the cost component. We can scale our resources as per our changing requirements from time to time. This provides an instant availability of practically infinite amount of cost-effective and quality computing infrastructure at our disposal. As the provisioning and monitoring are done centrally, and resources are maintained redundantly in geographically-distributed locations, cloud model is capable of offering highly available and reliable IT resources to consumers. Moreover, perceived security threats are actually at a much lesser scale when we take into account the data stored and software used across different user devices in varied business cycles with traditional IT processes.

Being a model gaining momentum along with rapidly evolving technologies, cloud computing provides enormous opportunities and challenges to service providers, engineers, consultants, developers and researchers.

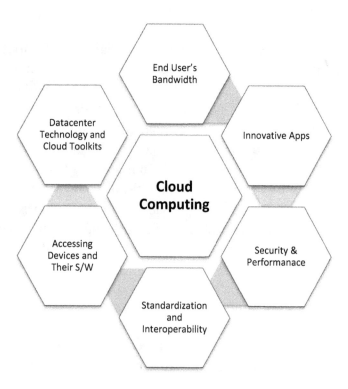

[Figure 7.1: Opportunities and Challenges of Cloud Computing]

Now, let us look at some of the opportunities and challenges offered by cloud computing (figure 7.1).

Innovative Apps

Software application architects and developers have a bigger opportunity to leverage the scenario where they do not get engaged in setting up environment, database management and other nitty-gritty tasks of software cycle management. All these are made available along with cloud platform, and moreover these can be managed with either high-end tools, or a set of APIs. And, there is a great need for creating new Apps for different usages.

HTML5 and JavaScript are gradually inching towards being the de facto languages for building Apps that are compatible across different devices and operating systems. With such probable convergence and the ease of creating Apps using cloud APIs would definitely increase the number and quality of Apps in near future.

There are a few major areas where rapid developments are happening. People would prefer to manage home appliances and other tools remotely, and integrating varied activities from a single device. As we have pointed earlier too, context-aware technologies and location-based computing would be used predominantly for building new Apps.

On the providers' side, there is a great demands on Apps to have better security controls, user management, cloud cost tracking, multi-currency support, audit controls and reporting, monitoring and alerting, auto-scaling, cloud bursting, backup management, and change management. In fact, further efforts are needed for unified cross-cloud management.

Security and Performance

A definite complaint that you would hear while talking about cloud computing is the security. In fact, periodic media flashes with sensational news about security breaches on leading cloud systems have strengthened such perceptions. A question mark is drawn on the capability of cloud vendors to ensure security for user data that are stored on their platforms. Moreover, the obvious consequence of storing private data on public cloud is seen as a perception of insecurity. Enterprises fear of taking on-premise data to public cloud where they share platform and resources with other enterprises or organizations. To let such perception be handled with our mundane minds, let us discuss an interesting example.

During 16th century, Golconda fort near Hyderabad, India, was one of the strongest forts which remained undefeated for long. However, the fort cannot stand the minimal warfare tactics of today. So, the parameters of security evolve as the technology and offense tactics improve or change. This implies that "being secured" is a relative perception that will change with time, and cannot be absolute. Other aspect of this example is how Moghul King Aurangzeb won over the Golconda fort. The history says the chieftain in charge of the door of fort opened it for the attackers in the middle of night in exchange of bribe and a promise of the throne. This aspect points to a situation where security was easily compromised by the people in charge, and it is due to their irresponsibility or intention. Thus the phrase of "being secured" is a perception we live with, and is not an absolute thing.

I believe that the above simple example tells the deeper story about security in general. The same can well be applied to IT security. Major threats come from within the organization; and the perception of being secured must be conveyed well by the provider. At the same time, the technical aspects of security must be taken care of; and adequate amount of research, monitoring and upgrade effort and cost must be dedicated for the purpose. In short, the sense of security must be retained among the users, and all technical and strategic efforts must be made on vendor side.

And now about performance. The major performance concerns when one or more components of cloud system fail to be available or accessible. This can be a simple loss of connectivity of central cloud components from the user device, or can be a situation where a particular App fails to respond successfully while fulfilling a user request. We have already discussed about handling such disconnected operations in Chapter 4; and this is an active area of development and research.

Standardization and Interoperability

Through Chapter 3, while making our point in favor of cloud computing, and in chapter 5, while discussing about the factors influencing cloud adoption, we have spoken at length of requirements of complying to the process of standardization of technologies and tools involved, and to facilitate data interoperability across platforms. However, complexity creeps into making decisions about specific vendors and usage patterns around different cloud systems due to varied yet less-compatible technology standards offered by respective vendors. Also, a growing set of consumers get locked with respective cloud platforms after they choose to use those. Similar is the case for solution providers who develop their solutions around a particular cloud ecosystem. Though the ecosystem around each offering seems to be expanding, the fears of being locked to particular vendors and lack of simplicity during various usage scenarios loom large on the consumers' side.

When we scan different enterprises, a clear division of interest groups for cloud adoption is seen among those who are already using legacy IT systems and others who are new. For existing IT users, the major task in the process of migration lies in transferring data to or using the data on the new ecosystem. This task can only be made redundant if the new system can facilitate interoperability and loose-coupling with different vendor platforms.

The current trend suggests consolidation in Industry along the NIST definition.

Accessing Devices and Their Software

Unfortunately, different vendors have approached hardware and software development in their own stride by focusing on creating tightly integrated platforms and Apps around those. This discourages end-users who have to adapt to new usage models each time they choose a new App or device from a new vendor. The technology landscape has been divided into virtually isolated monolithic ecosystems similar to farming lands split into small pieces through family inheritance.

Though there may not be any quick change in this scenario, we expect a standard App usage model across devices, and easy integration and porting between different platforms and devices in near future.

Datacenter Technologies and Cloud Toolkits

We have discussed about datacenters and the relevant technologies in our discussion in Chapter 4. While speaking on the changing demands from datacenters and their users, we have emphasized on two seemingly contradicting objectives like better reliability and lesser cost. But this is the reality; and there is a need to improve on technological aspects to achieve these competing goals.

The future innovations in this front will see emphasis on robust physical infrastructure along with higher-level of automation on infrastructure delivery cycle. This includes further development in cloud toolkits apart from other infrastructure related components.

Cost and Availability of Bandwidth

It would be deceiving if we do not account for the available bandwidth on the side of end-users and the cost involved. It is of no use if we end up spending more for bandwidth even though the cloud resources are available at cheaper cost. Thus there is a great requirement for technological advancements that will facilitate lowering the bandwidth costs and increasing the availability of higher bandwidth for end-users.

Conclusion

We are now heading towards the end of this book. We have discussed about cloud computing and the challenges/opportunities it has created for us. In fact, it is an open frontier in the realm of our technological endeavor.

Ubiquity of information technology and multitude of usage scenarios on one hand, and issues of consistency, availability and security on the other make this area an interesting study. As enormous effort has been made from different quarters to bring benefits of IT to global populace, it is pertinent to understand this new paradigm in detail; and it will enable us to adopt solutions in rightful manner, and also to maximize the benefits.

In spite of significant hypes, cloud computing is not an overnight phenomenon. Rather, it has taken several years to reach its current state through complex interplay of demands by users and innovations by service providers to meet the expectations from users. Though it has received wide visibility and has started establishing itself as an inseparable way of IT consumption, the evolution is still on; and more surprising impacts from this amazing computing paradigm cannot be ruled out.

Now my take...

Do not be limited in your thinking about the existing technologies or even their conceptual frameworks. Rather, we must be bold enough to appreciate the ground realities about the current state of progress, to extend the horizon to make technologies usable, and to bring newer technologies into the fold.

REFERENCE AND FURTHER READING

Please find the list of important references (books, magazine issues, articles, website links) that will help you expand your knowledge about the topics covered in this book. You can also refer to the book's website,

https://www.batoi.com/press/books/cloud-computing/

for updates, information about newer editions, and other resources to help you in your learning efforts.

History of IT and Cloud Computing:

- The Name Cloud Computing:
  http://www.johnmwillis.com/cloud-computing/who-coined-the-phrase-cloud-computing/

- A history of cloud computing:
  http://www.computerweekly.com/feature/A-history-of-cloud-computing

- Danny Sullivan in the Search Engine Strategies Conference on August 09, 2006: http://www.google.com/press/podium/ses2006.html

- Memorandum For Members and Affiliates of the Intergalactic Computer Network: http://www.kurzweilai.net/memorandum-for-members-and-affiliates-of-the-intergalactic-computer-network

General Reading on Cloud Computing:

- Cloud Computing on Wikipedia: http://en.wikipedia.org/wiki/Cloud_computing

- The NIST Definition of Cloud Computing: http://csrc.nist.gov/publications/nistpubs/800-145/SP800-145.pdf

- Rackspace Cloud University: http://www.rackspace.com/knowledge_center/cloudu/

- Cloud Computing Infographics: http://www.thecloudinfographic.com/

- "Executive's Guide to Cloud Computing" by Eric A. Marks and Bob Lozano; Published by John Wiley & Sons, Inc.; ISBN: 978-0-470-52172-4

- "Handbook of Cloud Computing" published by Springer; ISBN: 978-1-441-96523-3

- "Cloud Computing: Implementation, Management, and Security" by John W. Rittinghouse and James F.

Ransome; published by CRC Press (Taylor & Francis Group); ISBN: 978-1-4398-0680-7

- "Cloud Computing: Web-Based Applications that Change the Way You Work and Collaborate Online" by Michael Miller; published by QUE; ISBN: 978-0-7897-3803-5

Research and Survey Reports on Cloud Adoption and Strategies:

- Gartner's Hype Cycle for emerging technologies published in 2011:
  http://www.gartner.com/it/page.jsp?id=1763814

- High-Priority Requirements to Further USG Agency Cloud Computing Adoption:
  http://www.nist.gov/itl/cloud/upload/SP_500_293_volumeI-2.pdf

- Has Cloud Computing Matured – A Global Survey by Avanade:
  http://www.avanade.com/Documents/Research%20and%20Insights/FY11_Cloud_Exec_Summary.pdf

- Cloud Adoption Study by CIOnet:
  http://blog.cionet.com/wp-content/uploads/2011/10/Cloud-Adoption-Survey-2011.pdf

- State of Cloud Computing in Public Sector:
  http://www.frost.com/prod/servlet/cio/232651119

- USA Federal Strategy for Safe and Secure Adoption of Cloud Computing: http://www.apptis.com/documents/2011%20U.S.%2 0Federal%20Strategy%20for%20the%20Safe%20an d%20Secure%20Adoption%20of%20Cloud%20Com puting.pdf

- Balakrishna Narasimhan and Ryan Nichols. March 2011. State of Cloud Applications and Platforms: The Cloud Adopters' View. Computer, IEEE Computer Society

- Cloud Computing Adoption Risks: State of Play by Paul L. Bannerman: http://nicta.academia.edu/PaulBannerman/Papers/1 127346/Cloud_Computing_Adoption_Risks_State_ of_Play

- Carbon Disclosure project Study 2011: http://www.gesi.org/LinkClick.aspx?fileticket=q2BS piHHhS8%3D&tabid=216

- Cloud Computing Strategies by Dr. Dimitris N. Chorafas; Published by CRC Press (Taylor & Francis Group); ISBN: 978-1-439-83453-4

- Using Cloud Computing in Higher Education: A Strategy to Improve Agility in the Current Financial Crisis: http://www.ibimapublishing.com/journals/CIBIMA/ 2011/875547/875547.pdf

- 25 Point Implementation Plan to Reform Federal Information Technology Management:

http://www.cio.gov/documents/25-Point-Implementation-Plan-to-Reform-Federal%20IT.pdf

Datacenters, Virtualization and Cloud Orchestration:

- Automated Provisioning and Orchestration Is Critical to Effective Private Cloud Operations: http://www.cisco.com/en/US/prod/collateral/netmg tsw/ps6505/ps11869/idc_private_clouds.pdf

- Industry Trends and Vision: Evolution towards Datacenter Virtualization and private Cloud: http://www.brocade.com/downloads/documents/tec hnical_briefs/DataCenter_Virtualization_GA-TB-277-00.pdf

- Cloud Computing: Architecting a Microsoft Private Cloud: http://technet.microsoft.com/en-us/magazine/hh127072.aspx

- "Single-chip Cloud Computer" project: http://techresearch.intel.com/ProjectDetails.aspx?Id=1

Application Development on Cloud:

- "Code in the Cloud: Programming Google App Engine" by Mark C. Chu-Carroll; published by The Pragmatic Bookshelf; ISBN: 978-1-934356-63-0

- "PHP Development in the Cloud" by Ivo Jansch & Vito Chin; published by Blue Parabola; ISBN: 978-0-9810345-2-2

- "HOST YOUR WEB SITE IN THE CLOUD: AMAZON WEB SERVICES MADE EASY" by Jeff Barr; published by SitePoint Pty Ltd; ISBN: 978-0-9805768-3-2

- "Development with the Force.com Platform" by Jason Ouellette; published by Addison-Wesley; ISBN: 978-0-321-76735-6

- Cloud Tools: http://www.rackspace.com/cloud/tools/

- NoSQL Databases: http://nosql-database.org/

- Developing cloud apps: What's different: http://www.infoworld.com/d/cloud-computing/developing-cloud-apps-whats-different-675

ABOUT THE AUTHOR

A techno-entrepreneur innovator and writer, Ashwini Rath is the Founder Director & CEO at BATOI Systems (P) Limited (https://www.batoi.com). His current interests include semantic web, cloud computing and self-healing information architecture. Ashwini is a strong believer of knowledge-based socio-economic development. He lives with parents, wife and son; and loves Nature and Indian rural life.

Website of Author: http://ashwinirath.com

ABOUT BATOI PRESS

A modern publishing division providing services to authors and researchers. BATOI Press promotes knowledge-sharing among students, professionals and common people through e-books, audio-visual books, and research reports.

Website: https://www.batoi.com/press